CALYPSO BEAN SOUP

DATE		

CALYPSO BEAN SOUP

AND OTHER SAVORY RECIPES FEATURING
HEIRLOOM BEANS FROM THE WEST

Lesa Heebner

CollinsPublishersSanFrancisco
An Imprint of HarperCollins*Publishers*

A TREE CLAUSE BOOK

CollinsSanFrancisco and the author, in association with The Basic Foundation, a not-for-profit organization whose primary mission is reforestation, will facilitate the planting of two trees for every one tree used in the manufacture of this book.

Thanks to Zürsun Seeds of Ketchum, Idaho, for donating the bean seeds for the cover photo.

HarperCollins Web Site: http://www.harpercollins.com

HarperCollins®, 🏭®, CollinsPublishersSanFrancisco™, and A Tree Clause Book® are trademarks of HarperCollins Publishers Inc.

FIRST EDITION

Illustrations © Diana Reiss.
Book design by Claudia Smelser.

Library of Congress Cataloging-in-Publication Data:

Heebner, Lesa.
    Calypso bean soup : and other savory recipes featuring heirloom beans from the west/ Lesa Heebner.
     ISBN 0–06–258617–3 (pbk.)
     1. Soups.   2. Cookery (Beans).   3. Beans—Heirloom varieties—West (U.S.).   I. Title.
    TX757.H44   1996
    641.8'13—dc20   95–48279

96 97 98 99 00 ❖ RRD(H) 10 9 8 7 6 5 4 3 2 1

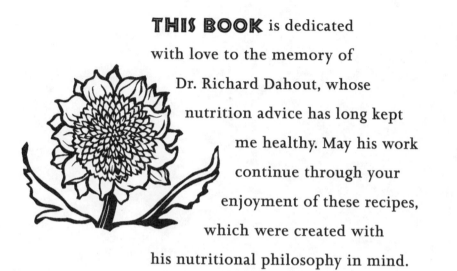

THIS BOOK is dedicated
with love to the memory of
Dr. Richard Dahout, whose
nutrition advice has long kept
me healthy. May his work
continue through your
enjoyment of these recipes,
which were created with
his nutritional philosophy in mind.

TABLE OF CONTENTS

OVEN-BAKED BEAN MAIN DISHES

ACKNOWLEDGMENTS

I spent many hours digging for scientific and historical information on the beans that grow in the western United States. The genealogy, legends, and lore I found fascinated me! I was amazed again by the "pull" that foods have on the history of humankind, and by the individual efforts that make up that historical force—the shadows behind the stories, the men and women who carried, planted, harvested, cooked, and served the beans. I am grateful for their respect for tradition and their tremendous efforts to preserve it.

Thank you to all the people who shared their knowledge with me, including Dr. Steve Temple of the University of California at Davis; Dr. Joe Mogga and Dr. Mark Brick at Colorado State University at Fort Collins; Dr. Tom Lumpkin and Dr. Barry Swanson at Washington State University at Pullman; Dr. Rich Hannan, head of the Western Regional Plant Introduction Station at Washington State University at Pullman; Dr. Matt Silbernagle at Washington State University at Prosser and the United States Department of Agriculture; Dr. Jim Kelley and Dr. Mark Uebersax at Michigan State University; Dr. Dermot P. Coyne at the University of Nebraska at Lincoln; Elizabeth Berry of Gallina Canyon Ranch; Linda Prim of Abiquiu, New Mexico; Loretta Barrett Oden, owner of the Corn Dance Cafe in Santa Fe, New Mexico; ethnobotanist Liná Austin of Phoenix, Arizona; L. L. "Bill" Dean of the Idaho Bean Seed Company; Ken Rauch of The Bean Bag; Bruce Riddell of Adobe Milling Company; Lola Weyman of Zürsun Ltd.; Valerie Phipps of Phipps Ranch; Kevin Dahl of Native Seeds/SEARCH; Howard Shapiro of Seeds of Change; and Gary Paul Nabhan for his wonderful books, especially *Enduring Seeds: Native American Agriculture and Wild Plant Conservation* (North Point Press, San Francisco, 1989).

A big thank-you to Annie Rippo VeneKlasen for her hours of helping me test and retest these recipes, to Laura Ann Thompson for steering me to a number of great bean sources, and to friend and local grower Mary Culver for planting many of the varieties of heirloom beans I cooked with in this book.

To my agent, Julie Castiglia, thank you for helping me through this one, too! To dear friend and colleague Betz Collins, thank you for all your sage advice. To Lynn Edmundson and Sally Guenther, as always, thank you for being there for me. And to my husband, Don Davis, thank you for your love and support. I am forever grateful you are in my life.

INTRODUCTION

Long known as "poor man's food," the lowly bean is now tantalizing those of us who are intrigued with its many colorful varieties—some speckled or mottled, others deeply hued or pure white. Even their names evoke adventure. What legends lie behind the names of Indian Woman yellow beans, painted pony, calypso, or Anasazi® beans? Pinto, navy, and Great Northern beans, quite common to the American table, also have fascinating backgrounds. In fact, their histories, or tales of their rediscovery, are tinged with romance. Some were carried with care by immigrants to their new land, others said to be found in pottery at the sites of ancient civilizations. Some are simply genetic "slips" with markings and flavors appealing enough to save them. And many more beans were part of the dietary culture of every Native American tribe who farmed the land throughout the Americas. We're captivated by their color, their history, and their mystery—what did the ancient peoples know about this food that we don't?

Today, there is a strong movement to preserve the seeds of these beans and other foodstuffs of our past. Seed-saving foundations exist in the Southwest, Midwest, and East. Their mission is to secure the diversity and quality of our food supply by maintaining the seeds of the many plants our ancestors grew. Why is this necessary? Because the needs of agribusiness—the conglomerate growers—are drastically changing the nature and availability of our food supply. These growers want high-yield, pest-resistant, uniform crops—variety, taste, and texture are not high on their wish lists. Research at agricultural colleges and other research centers focuses on "designing" plants to meet these big-business needs. The seed savers, however, are perpetuating the desirable "old-fashioned" traits, like full flavor and tender skins, found in the plants of our forebears. And they are preserving the multiple varieties of plants—not just one "super-bean," for instance—necessary to maintain our food supply, and thus our long-term health. Over the centuries, humans have used almost three thousand plants for food. Maybe 150 have been grown on a commercial basis. Today, the number of major food crops is much smaller—85 percent to 90 percent of all food grown is derived from just fifteen plants. Thomas Jefferson once said that "the greatest service which can be rendered any country is to add a useful plant to its culture." To save foods and preserve our food heritage, then, is at least a patriotic act, if not a humanitarian effort.

In days past, seeds were saved by families and passed down from generation to generation. This is a typical story from the *Seed Savers Exchange: The First Ten Years* annual. A bean, which came to be known as the Mostoller bean, and by future generations as the "wild goose bean," came to the Mostoller family in a strange way, which endeared it to the family for years to come. During the time of the Civil War, the family ran a mill on Stoneycreek, near Bedford County, Pennsylvania. One fall, when the ducks and geese were migrating, severe weather caused a number of these waterfowl to land on Stoneycreek. One of the geese ventured into the channel of water that drives the mill wheel, and so one of the Mostoller brothers, viewing this as a windfall dinner, shot the goose. They got more dinners than they ever imagined out of this goose. After it had been plucked, a good look revealed a very distended craw. It contained a large number of beans, which were removed and placed on the windowsill to dry. That spring, they were planted, and have continued to feed Mostoller family and friends for 124 years.

Seed-saving foundations now receive many seeds that have been preserved and grown by families for generations. Some are still grown by the family, while other families have found their time limited, and so may no longer grow the seeds. Many of them do want the seeds preserved, so they send them to seed-saving foundations, which preserve and grow them out every few years in their large, volunteer-tended gardens. The majority of this seed is then sold to home gardeners. But some is sold to small-scale commercial farmers—I call them "boutique" growers—most of which are located in the western United States. They make their products available to consumers through mail-order catalogs. See "Sources for Beans and Seeds," page 91, for information on where to send for these beans, both to cook and to grow.

Additionally, the United States Department of Agriculture maintains seed banks. Thankfully, under the direction of Dr. Richard Hannan, the Western Regional Plant Introduction Station in Pullman, Washington, has recently begun the effort to collect and save family-heritage beans.

Many of the beans in this book are grown by boutique growers from "heritage" or "heirloom" seeds. Of course, I've included the names of more commonly known beans in the Substitution Chart (page xxv), that can be successfully substituted for the heritage beans. I predict, however, that the beans presented here will be more readily available in the next few years because of their beauty, flavor, texture, and our increased awareness of how important these heritage beans are to our future. Additionally, gourmet restaurants, especially in the West and Southwest, are catching on to the appeal of these beans because of their fresh taste, a quality not usually associated with dried legumes. Much like the chile craze, beans are just beginning their reign as the food darling of the 1990s.

Besides being associated with Western tradition, beans are ever-present in the West because of the favorable growing conditions. Growers like the long, sunny seasons that provide consistently high-quality crops. Of greatest importance, there is predictably no rain at harvesttime. If wet, beans can easily rot; and if dried when wet, they have proven to be too hard to cook, and are so discolored the crop is essentially lost.

Even the nutritional numbers look good. Beans are high in the good things—protein, carbohydrates, iron, fiber, and B vitamins—and low in the bad things—fat, cholesterol, and sodium. If you're at all interested in good health, beans are very attractive indeed.

Despite all these positive attributes—beauty, health, adventure, tradition, versatility—beans have an unsavory reputation. They will always be known for one thing. They make a fuss on the way out. But we now know ways to lessen this problem and make bean consumption completely appealing. See "How to Silence Beans," page xvii, for all the details.

BEANS AT THEIR BEST

This book is a collection of original recipes that incorporates those details, on how to silence beans, using familiar, as well as the new-to-us but very old, beans of the western United States. The solution to beans' well-known problem is to prepare them in proper combinations. You will therefore not find any "chuckwagon-type" recipes with brown sugar and molasses. Instead, there are lighter, prettier creations such as soups of beans and greens seasoned with garden-fresh stock, salads topped with garbanzo "croutons," and gratins baked to creamy perfection. My beans are accented with pasilla chiles, wasabi, and garden-fresh herbs such as tarragon and basil; they are topped with feta cheese, wrapped in phyllo or wontons, and sauced with vegetable and herb purées. It's a new approach to a very old food. Come with me as I blaze a fresh trail through the old frontier.

HOW TO SILENCE BEANS

Why do beans cause so much gastric distress? There are three reasons, two of which are fairly well known. First, the human digestive system does not have the enzyme needed to metabolize the complex sugars, called oligosaccharides, found in beans. We can only digest simple sugars. So when we eat beans, the complex sugars pass from the upper intestine undigested into the lower intestine where the bacteria there begin to go to work on them. The bacteria can't gobble them up; they can only break them down via fermentation, which results in hydrogen, methane, and carbon dioxide gases.

There are a number of things you can do that will effectively lessen the repercussions of these troublesome sugars. First, soak beans before you cook them. Seventy-five to 90 percent of the complex sugars are thrown out with the soaking water. Soak them overnight in enough water to cover them plus a few spare inches. Or quick-soak them by adding the beans to a pot. Cover them with water, plus a few extra inches, cover the pot, bring to a boil, turn the heat off, and let sit for one and a half to four hours. Always drain off the soaking water, and begin cooking with fresh water. Soaking has the added benefit of shortening the cooking time substantially.

Second, there is a product on the market called Bean-O, made by AK Pharma, Inc. It is made of the enzyme that will digest these complex sugars. Add a few drops to your first bite of beans. Even though this makes perfect sense, results are mixed—it works for some, but not all.

Another way to cope with the complex sugars is to add a strip of kombu seaweed, found at natural food stores and Oriental groceries, to each pot of beans for the first hour of cooking. Then remove and discard it. Not only is kombu seaweed very effective for aiding digestion of beans, it adds valuable trace minerals and antioxidants to the diet. It's unclear why kombu works, but it may be the presence of high levels of potassium, without sugars, that stimulate the gastric juices and promote more effective digestion.

The fourth way you can temper the effects of beans' complex sugars is to eat them more often. In cultures where beans are eaten daily, cooks don't even soak their beans and never complain about gas (the advantages, besides the obvious, are a stronger flavor to the beans, and no loss of the water-soluble vitamins—you do discard some with the soaking water). Many research scientists, and bean commissions all over the country, agree—eat beans more often, and the bacteria that ferments these oligosaccharides "gets used to" the sugars and doesn't cause as much gas.

Besides the oligosaccharides, the second reason beans cause gas is their fiber content. Beans have two fibers, which is actually something to boast about. Soluble fiber, made famous by oat bran, helps lower blood cholesterol and stabilize blood sugar levels. Insoluble fiber, like miller's bran, is the type that keeps you regular. But many people do not consume enough fiber of either kind, so when they eat the fiber-loaded bean, or any other food with fiber for that matter, they experience gastric distress. Add more of all kinds of fiber to your diet—fruits, vegetables, and grains—and beans will be less of a problem.

The third reason beans cause gas is because each bean is a little bundle of protein plus carbohydrates. Beans range between one and three parts carbohydrate to every part protein. This is wonderful for us because we can use the carbohydrates for energy and the protein for building tissue. However, we face a problem when we try to digest them.

Proteins and carbohydrates require different pH levels to get through our systems. Protein asks for a much lower pH, or a more acidic environment, to break it down. Carbohydrates want a pH over 4.0, or a more alkaline environment, in which to break down. When proteins and carbohydrates arrive at the same time, as in the case with all beans, a little trouble results. Chewing begins the digestion process—no problems here. Then an enzyme in our mouths, salivary amylase, begins to break down the carbohydrates. No problem for a little while. The drama starts when the amylase becomes inactivated because of the protein's need for an acidic environment. In effect, the salivary amylase is neutralized by the acid of the gastric secretions called upon by the protein. Starch digestion is put on hold until the protein is broken down, at which time the acidic environment must be transformed into its opposite, an alkaline one, to digest the remaining starches. The stomach recognizes these two warring factions, and under ideal conditions—no stress, no illness, no injury, no worn-out parts—eventually works it all out.

But obviously, a little gastric distress results along the way. Is there anything we can do to curtail it? Yes. We can choose to combine beans with foods that will not put additional stress on an already taxed digestion process, and in fact will help the process along.

WAYS TO MAKE BEANS FRIENDLY

With three sources of gastric distress from beans, there are numerous effective actions to take. As discussed, to combat the problems associated with beans' complex sugars, soak them in water, add Bean-O, and/or cook with kombu. To deal with the fiber, eat beans more often, and to get around the conflicting digestive needs of proteins and starches, be careful of what you eat with beans.

The best foods to eat in combination with beans are vegetables. The parasympathetic nervous system controls digestion. The more relaxed, the better it works. All vegetables are high in potassium and enzymes, which relax the stomach and aid digestion. A meal with beans and vegetables is light, easier to handle, and something new and different for bean cuisine. Something you may want more often.

Probably the worst combination is beans with fruit or sugar. Like vegetables, there is potassium in fruit, but there's also plenty of sugar, which the body reads as simple starch. This starch puts immediate demands on the body's systems—but remember, starch has to wait until the protein is digested—so digestion simply can't keep up. Want a bloated stomach? Eat a bowl of beans with raisins, then have dessert.

When beans and meat are eaten together, protein is concentrated dramatically, which imposes a huge workload on the stomach. Imagine the amount of acid called upon to digest all that protein! And then comes the challenge of switching gears completely to create an alkaline environment for the starches. To be kinder, be content with the protein in the beans alone. If you must add meat to a meal with beans, add very small amounts. When beans and grains are eaten together, it's a little easier on our systems. The acid needs aren't so high, so switching to alkaline is not so imposing a task.

It's also interesting to note that, generally, the smaller the bean, the less carbohydrate it contains, so the easier it is to digest.

If you take all the steps recounted here, beans will no longer be a digestive challenge, and you can feel free to enjoy them—silently—in all the delicious recipes in this book.

BASICS

TO SOAK BEANS, choose one of two methods. The method known as the "long soak" is best known. Put beans into a bowl, cover them with water (plus a spare couple of inches so the beans remain covered with water as they plump), and let them soak for eight hours, or overnight. The "quick soak" method is just as effective, and great for those of us who don't plan meals a day in advance. Put the beans in the pot you will eventually cook them in. Cover with water, plus a spare couple of inches, cover the pot, bring to a boil, then turn the heat off, and let sit for one and a half to four hours. Both methods rehydrate a dehydrated vegetable, thus shortening cooking time. Additionally, soaking helps prevent digestive distress.

TO TELL WHEN BEANS HAVE SOAKED ENOUGH, pierce one with your thumbnail. If the bean resists, and feels a little like glass, they have not soaked enough. But if your thumbnail can penetrate easily, they're ready to be rinsed and cooked.

BEFORE COOKING THE BEANS always drain the soaking water and start with fresh water. If you live in an area with a high mineral content in the water, use bottled water to cook your beans. The minerals inhibit the beans from softening.

ADD A SIX-INCH STRIP OF KOMBU SEAWEED to every two cups of dried beans for the first hour of cooking to help eliminate the gas associated with eating beans. See page xvii for a more thorough discussion.

TO ENSURE THAT YOUR BEANS SOFTEN, do not add tomatoes, vinegar, citrus juice, or wine to the pot for the first one to one and a half hours. Beans will not soften if acidic ingredients are initially added to the cooking water. Salt is a controversial subject. Some people say it too prevents the beans from softening; others say it doesn't and that furthermore, salting initially gives the beans extra flavor. I prefer to salt the beans after they have softened. The age of beans is also a factor in this equation. Buy your beans from stores with a high turnover so you are assured your beans aren't so old they won't soften. Additionally, improper storage will prevent beans from softening. Do not store at high temperatures or in high humidity.

TO ROAST BELL PEPPERS AND POBLANO CHILES, preheat the oven to Broil. Cut the peppers in half lengthwise, remove and discard seeds and veins, and place, cut-side down, on a lightly oiled cookie sheet. Broil until blackened. Remove from the cookie sheet to a bowl. Cover with a plate to let the peppers steam in their own heat, which will help loosen the darkened skin. When cool enough to handle, peel away the darkened skin. Use gloves when peeling poblanos so the capsaicin (pepper) oil doesn't burn your hands.

TO ROAST ANAHEIM CHILES, proceed as above if you have an electric stove. If you have a gas stove, remove the grate from one burner. Turn the heat to high, and place anaheims directly in the flame, turning frequently, until they are completely charred. Remove and discard the blackened skin, stem, seeds, and veins (use gloves so the pepper oil doesn't burn your hands).

TO ROAST GARLIC CLOVES, preheat the oven to 350°F. Put individual garlic cloves, skins on, on a baking sheet and bake for twenty to thirty minutes, or until soft.

TO MAKE ANCHO, PASILLA, NEW MEXICO, OR GUAJILLO CHILE POWDER, preheat the oven to 200°F. Remove stems, seeds, and veins from the dried chiles (wear gloves). Place on a cookie sheet and bake for one hour. The chiles will become brittle once they are removed from the oven. Put the chiles in the work bowl of a food processor and process to a powder. Store extra chile powder in empty spice bottles or resealable plastic bags. Chile powder will keep for up to one year.

TO PEEL AND SEED TOMATOES, fill a large pasta pot with water and bring to a boil. Slice a small cross into the bottom of each tomato. Drop each into the boiling water for ten seconds. Remove and rinse with cold water. Peel off the skin, starting where you made the cross. Cut in half cross-wise and squeeze out the seeds.

TO MAKE ROASTED TOMATO PURÉE, preheat the oven to 325°F. Cut the tomatoes in half crosswise. Place on a cookie sheet, cut-side up. Spray the tops lightly with olive oil spray, and bake for one and a half hours. While still hot, purée in a food processor. One pound of tomatoes makes three-fourths cup purée.

TO MAKE SHERRIED TOMATO PASTE, pour a half cup of sherry over one cup of sundried tomatoes. Heat in the microwave for two minutes or on the stove top for ten minutes, then let sit to soften about twenty minutes. Put the sherry and tomatoes in the work bowl of a food processor and process. Add two to four tablespoons of water as needed to process into a paste. Makes two-thirds cup sherried tomato paste, or about ten tablespoons. Cover and refrigerate. It will keep for up to one month.

TO MAKE YOGURT CHEESE, put nonfat plain yogurt in a yogurt drainer or coffee filter suspended over a glass. (Choose a brand of yogurt without gelatin—gelatin prevents the separation of whey from "curds.") Let the yogurt drain at least one hour, or refrigerate and drain overnight. The longer it drains, the thicker and richer the resulting yogurt cheese will be.

SUBSTITUTION CHART

To simplify substitution of more available beans for the less common heritage ones, I've divided all beans into five basic categories based on color, which relates to taste.* The more color a bean has, the more flavor. Use any bean in that column to substitute for another in that same color/flavor category. Those beans in parentheses can only be substituted in certain instances, as noted in the recipes. Please note that when a recipe calls for flageolet or garbanzo beans, it is wise to use only them as no other bean duplicates their taste and textural nuances.

SMALL WHITE	LARGE WHITE	MILD BEIGE	STRONG BEIGE	BLACK
rice beans	Great Northern	pinto	buckskin	calypso
garboncito/ China yellow	Hopi woman/ pueblo/mortgage lifters/Aztec white	Anasazi®	Indian Woman yellow	Mitla
small lima	cannellini	rattlesnake	borlotti/ improved cranberry pinquito	kidney
white tepary	small or large lima	New Mexico appaloosa	golden tepary	(lentils)
black-eyed peas	garboncito/ China yellow	red appaloosa	cranberry	(Anasazi®)
small white	snowcap	appaloosa	(lentils)	
navy	small white	painted pony/ brown mare		
	navy	bolita butterscotch calypso/ yellow eye		

---

* As an aside, it is interesting to note that the protein quality in colored beans is less than in white beans. Protein is tied up with the tannins, or color compounds, and when bound together, can't be thoroughly digested, thus less is available nutritionally.

EQUIVALENCIES

1 cup dried beans equals 2 to 3 cups cooked beans.

1 cup dried beans equals 1 to 1¼ pounds cooked beans.

1 cup dried beans equals approximately 4 servings.

2 cups dried beans equals approximately 1 pound (dry weight).

One 16-ounce can beans equals approximately 1½ cups cooked.

CALYPSO BEAN SOUP

Bean Appetizers and Side Dishes

GREAT NORTHERN BEAN AND ALMOND DIP

The common bean variety, which includes the Great Northern bean as well as the pinto, navy, black bean, and others, has been grown in the Americas since as early as 6000 B.C. The common bean is unique in that it has two geographic centers of origin: the Andean, which is near the Andes Mountains of Peru, and the Mesoamerican, which includes Mexico and South America. In other words, people were growing and developing different types of the common bean at the same time in two locations. Other foods, for instance the tomato, typically originated in just one place. Through trading and travel, beans made their way north through the Americas, where different tribes of Native Americans grew small patches of beans for their own consumption, selecting and developing varieties based on taste, climate, and pest and disease resistance.

The original Great Northern bean seed was given to a man named Oscar H. Will in 1897 by Son of Star, a Hidatsa Indian, whose tribe raised the beans for many years. Will increased its number and sold it in his catalog through the 1940s. The University of Idaho then created a strain of Great Northern bean from the original Hidatsa bean that they called UI #59. It became the predominate Great Northern bean through the 1970s. From the 1980s until today, new varieties are constantly being derived through hybridization. Unfortunately, no one grows the original Great Northern bean that Son of Star gave Will, but there is some acreage, albeit small, of UI #59, the closest relative to the Hidatsa bean.

Great Northern beans won't flourish in the eastern United States, but they do grow quite successfully in the western states of Idaho, Colorado, Wyoming, and Nebraska. They have a mild flavor and cakey texture that makes them ideal for blending into a smooth paste with other ingredients. Almond butter, found at natural food stores and farmers' markets, is made like peanut butter, but from roasted almonds. It adds a mild, sweet flavor to this versatile dip. Serve cupped in a cabbage leaf with vegetable crudités and blue corn chips.

1 cup	dried Great Northern beans, soaked and rinsed, or two 16-ounce cans Great Northern beans
One 3-inch piece	kombu seaweed
1 clove	garlic, finely minced
¼ cup	fresh lime juice
¼ cup	almond butter
½ cup	fresh cilantro leaves
⅛ to ¼ teaspoon	cayenne
½ teaspoon	black pepper
	Salt, to taste
¼ cup	diced red onion

1 Put the beans, fresh water to cover by 2 inches, and kombu in a 3- or 4-quart saucepan. Cover, bring to a boil, reduce the heat, and simmer, covered, for 1 hour. Remove the kombu and cook for 30 to 60 minutes longer, or until the beans are tender. Or, rinse the canned beans.

2 Put the drained beans plus the garlic, lime juice, almond butter, cilantro, cayenne, and black pepper in the work bowl of a food processor. Process until smooth. Add salt as needed.

3 Transfer to a serving bowl. Stir in the diced red onion. Chill at least one hour to develop flavors.

4 Serve with blue corn chips, vegetable chips, carrot sticks, celery sticks, and other crudités.

Makes about 4 cups

BABY LIMA BEANS WITH PARSLEY PESTO

It had been thirty-three years since a lima bean touched my lips. Not since Uncle Jim made me sit in front of a plate of them until I ate every bite. Of course, I outlasted him, and I only had to swallow one "butter bean," as he called them, before I was excused from the table. I never considered eating another until about a year ago when my curiosity got the best of me. I bought a bag of baby limas, not yet brave enough to attempt the large ones. They were a pleasant surprise—didn't taste at all like the "slimy bug" I remember swallowing at age five. In fact, for dried beans, they taste very fresh to me. And tossed when hot with this lemony parsley pesto, they explode in your mouth with the liveliest flavor. Promise me, though—out of respect to the children we all once were—you won't force any kid to eat these.

BEANS

1½ cups	dried baby lima beans, soaked and drained
One 3-inch piece	kombu seaweed

PESTO

2 cloves	garlic
1½ cups	loosely packed parsley leaves
1 teaspoon	lemon zest
1 tablespoon	lemon juice
3 tablespoons	extra virgin olive oil
¼ cup	grated Parmesan cheese, preferably Reggiano Parmigiano

TO FINISH

	Salt and black pepper, to taste
Scant ⅛ teaspoon	cayenne

1   Put the beans, fresh water to cover by 2 inches, and kombu in a 3-
    or 4-quart saucepan. Cover, bring to a boil, reduce the heat, and sim-
    mer, covered, for 40 minutes, or until beans are tender yet still retain
    their shape. Remove and discard kombu.
2   While the beans simmer, make the pesto by putting garlic, parsley leaves,
    and lemon zest in the work bowl of a food processor or blender. Process
    until finely minced.
3   Add the lemon juice, oil, and cheese. Process until smooth.
4   When the lima beans are done, drain off the extra water, and toss with
    the pesto while still hot. Taste, and season with salt, black pepper, and
    cayenne. Serve hot, warm, or cold.

Serves 6

CANNELLINI BEANS AND BREAD, SPANISH-STYLE

The Spanish have the best way with bread. No basket of puffy white rolls with foil-covered frozen butter. They present a still life–quality tray of toasted bread, plus peeled cloves of raw garlic, halved fresh tomatoes, and a carafe of fruity olive oil. During my first trip to Spain I was instructed to scrape a piece of the raw garlic over the surface of the toast, rub the tomato over that, then dip the flavored bread in the olive oil. What follows is a heartier version of this incredible treat, with the addition of herb-spiked beans. You may also want to serve it with a mixed green salad for a small but satisfying dinner.

BEANS

1 cup	dried cannellini beans, soaked and drained, or two 16-ounce cans cannellini beans
One 3-inch strip	kombu seaweed
2 whole cloves	garlic, peeled
½ teaspoon	salt
½ teaspoon	dried rosemary, or 1 teaspoon minced fresh rosemary
½ cup	chopped fresh parsley or basil
1 tablespoon	extra virgin olive oil

BREAD

12 slices	sourdough bread
6 cloves	garlic, peeled and sliced in half
6	tomatoes, cut in half crosswise

1 Put the beans in a 3- or 4-quart saucepan. Add fresh water to cover by 2 inches, kombu, and garlic and cook for 1 hour or until the beans are tender. Remove and discard kombu. Or, rinse the canned beans.
2 Drain beans and mash a few beans, plus the garlic cloves, with a fork. Stir in salt, rosemary, parsley or basil, and olive oil, taste and adjust seasoning, then set aside until ready to serve.
3 Meanwhile, toast, broil, or grill bread.
4 To serve, rub the halved cloves of garlic on the toasted bread, then rub the halved tomatoes across the bread. Use the flavored bread as a "pusher" for the beans. Serve alongside a mixed green salad or as a side dish to a vegetarian meal.

Serves 6 to 12

RAJAS, PASILLA BUTTER, AND CALYPSO BEAN PINWHEELS

The calypso bean is a black and white bean with markings similar to the well-known yin-yang symbol. It was an oddball bean in a batch of black beans that slipped by, undetected by the electronic eye, but was spotted by an alert human eye. It was so attractive that the grower planted it, saved the seeds it generated, then grew those out until they had enough for acres of these unique beans. All told, it takes about three years to accumulate enough for a planting. The calypso bean is similar in flavor to, yet milder than, the black turtle bean, its progenitor.

This bean dish is made with *rajas*, which are strips of roasted chiles. They add tremendous flavor and texture to these attractive appetizers. Pasilla butter is a creamy blend of pasilla chile powder and yogurt that is spread onto steamed tortillas. Add a layer of the calypso beans, a sprinkling of shredded cheese, then roll it all up like a rug. Slice crosswise and you have pinwheels of flavor!

1 cup	dried calypso beans, soaked and rinsed
One 3-inch strip	kombu seaweed
2 whole cloves	garlic, peeled
½	yellow onion, quartered
1	carrot, cut into 2-inch chunks
½ teaspoon	salt
2	red bell peppers
2	anaheim chiles
1½ tablespoons	pasilla chile powder (see Basics chapter, page xxii)
3 tablespoons	nonfat plain yogurt
4	burrito-size flour tortillas
1 cup	shredded cheddar cheese
	Vegetable oil spray as needed
	Salsa as needed
	Yogurt cheese (see Basics chapter, page xxii) as needed (optional)

1 Put the beans in a 3- or 4-quart saucepan. Add the kombu, garlic, onion, carrot, and enough water to cover by 2 inches. Cover, bring to a boil, reduce the heat to low, and simmer for 45 to 60 minutes, until beans are tender. Remove and discard the kombu and vegetables. Stir in salt. Set aside until ready to assemble pinwheels.

2 See Basics chapter on how to roast the bell peppers and anaheim chiles, page xxii. To make rajas, slice peppers and chiles into strips and set aside.

3 Mix pasilla chile powder with yogurt to make pasilla butter and set aside.

4 Steam the tortillas until limp by wrapping them in moistened paper towels and microwaving them on high power for 2 minutes. (If you don't have a microwave, spray a nonstick skillet lightly with vegetable oil spray and cook the tortillas, turning once, until limp.)

5 To assemble, drain the beans and mash. Spread the pasilla butter over each of the steamed tortillas. Divide the rajas among the 4 tortillas. Add the grated cheese, then top with the mashed beans. Roll up each tortilla like you'd roll up a rug. The mashed beans will hold them closed.

6 To cook, lightly spray a nonstick skillet with vegetable oil spray. Heat to medium-high. Cook the rolled-up, filled tortillas until golden on all sides. Cut into eighths, using a serrated knife. When turned on their sides, they should resemble pinwheels. Assemble on a platter and top with a dollop of salsa and/or yogurt cheese. Serve hot, warm, or at room temperature.

Serves 8

GOLDEN TEPARY BEAN AND FETA CHEESE WONTONS WITH SALSA VERDE

Tepary beans are ancient beans grown in years past by Native Americans in the arid Southwest. They are one of the four species of *Phaseolus*, or beans indigenous to the Americas, and unfortunately the least known and grown, as they are quite delicious, especially if you like smaller beans as I do. Today they are not grown commercially, but the Pima and the Papago Indians cultivate them for their own tables. Tepary bean seed coats vary in color from white to golden to brown.

I prepare them here in an unconventional manner—wrapped in wontons. I justify this unlikely presentation with the beauty and enhanced flavors of the finished appetizer. Fold the wontons up over the filling to resemble bishop's hats, steam briefly so they're soft and pliable, and serve. If you don't want to take the time to wrap the wontons, use corn or flour tortillas instead—a more traditional approach. Smear half of each tortilla with the bean mixture, fold the tortilla over the filling, and brown in a nonstick skillet moistened with a little vegetable oil spray. Although delicious and moist enough on their own, you might want to serve either version of these appetizers with Salsa Verde, Green Chile Sauce (see recipes on pages 65 and 75), or your favorite brand of salsa.

1 cup	dried golden tepary beans, soaked and rinsed
One 3-inch strip	kombu seaweed
2 cloves	garlic, finely minced
½	yellow onion, quartered
½ teaspoon	salt
1 teaspoon	ground cumin
½ teaspoon	dried basil
2	scallions, sliced into rounds
2	large tomatoes, diced
½ cup	crumbled feta cheese
60	wonton wrappers
	Salsa Verde (see recipe, page 65) or Green Chile Sauce (see recipe, page 75) (optional)

1 Put the beans in a 3- or 4-quart saucepan. Add the kombu, garlic, onion, and enough water to cover by 2 inches. Cover, bring to a boil, reduce the heat to low, and simmer for 45 to 60 minutes, until the beans are tender. Remove and discard the kombu. Set aside until ready to assemble wontons.

2 Just before assembling wontons, drain and mash the beans, garlic, and onion with a fork or potato masher.

3 Add the salt, cumin, basil, scallions, tomatoes, and cheese to the beans and stir.

4 To assemble the wontons, place one wonton wrapper in the palm of your hand, one corner facing you. Add 1 tablespoon of the filling to the center of the wrapper. Moisten the 2 edges of the wrapper that are closest to the bottom of your hand with a little water. Fold the wrapper in half, forming a triangle. Press tightly to seal the entire edge. Moisten the 2 tips of the long edge of the triangle and press them together. As you finish the wontons, place them on a dinner plate in a single layer. You may cover and refrigerate wontons overnight, or cook them immediately.

5 To cook the wontons, line a steamer basket with lettuce leaves or parchment paper (this will prevent the wontons from sticking to the pan). Add wontons in a single layer and steam over boiling water for 4 minutes.

6 Serve hot, warm, or at room temperature with or without sauces.

Makes 60 wontons or 12 filled tortillas that can be cut into 3 pieces each.

FLAGEOLET BEANS PARMIGIANO

I adore flageolet beans because of their just-picked taste, so I was disappointed that I wouldn't be able to include them in this book of western beans—everyone knows they grow in Europe. Everyone, I guess, except the people in Idaho who grow them! The Idaho flageolets are shipped to purveyors in France and Italy, who sell them to their compatriots, and then package and ship a portion of them back to us! This well-traveled bean is the most expensive of all dried beans, and this is why. Purchase current-crop American stay-at-home flageolets from Zürsun Ltd. (see "Sources for Beans and Seeds," page 91).

Their "green" flavor is due to the fact that they are picked before they are fully ripe. They are very delicately flavored, so this simple preparation complements them completely.

2 cups	dried flageolet beans, soaked and drained
5 to 6 cups	chicken broth (3 or 4 cans)
One 6-inch strip	kombu seaweed
2	bay leaves
½ teaspoon	black pepper
	Salt, to taste
½ cup	freshly grated Reggiano Parmigiano
About ¼ cup	chopped fresh parsley leaves (optional)

1 Put the beans in a 3- or 4-quart saucepan. Add the chicken broth, kombu, and bay leaves. Cover, bring to a boil, reduce heat to low, and simmer for 60 minutes, until the beans are tender yet still hold their shape. Check to make sure they are covered with broth at all times. After 1 hour, remove and discard kombu and bay leaves.

2 When done, drain all but ½ cup of chicken broth. Add salt and pepper to taste.

3 Add the cheese and parsley to the beans while they're still hot and let sit for 10 to 15 minutes to absorb the broth and develop the flavors. Serve warm.

Serves 8 to 10 as a side dish

GARBONCITO BEANS WITH CARAMELIZED TOMATOES

A caramelized tomato is a powerhouse of flavor and texture. The process of slow baking tomatoes intensifies their sweetness, the longer baking time improves their texture over standard-baked tomatoes, and the additions of garlic and basil accent their agreeable flavor. The resulting caramelized tomatoes marry beautifully with any sweet or delicately flavored foods. Pair them with crusty slices of bread, thick strands of pasta, a bowl full of braised spinach leaves, steaming mounds of rice, or a pot of sweet garboncito beans.

Although *garboncito* means "little garbanzo" in Spanish, garboncitos are not mini-garbanzos, but an entirely different bean. It is said that the garboncitos derived their name from their visual similarity to the garbanzo, but I've looked and all I can see is that they're both round. Their differences far outnumber their similarities. The garboncito's buttery color differs from the garbanzo's pinkish hue. They are both round, but the garboncito is more uniform. Further, garboncitos were domesticated in Mexico rather than in the Middle East, as garbanzos were. And the garbanzo's distinctive meaty taste contrasts with the garboncito's mild nutty flavor. Go figure! There is also a smaller bean in Mexico called the *garboncito chico,* which is also not related. Maybe all round beans in Mexico were simply named after the garbanzo. Or perhaps they shared more common characteristics when they were first named, but as they were carried from one farm to another, one country to the next, their visual similarities were bred out in favor of increased flavor or disease resistance. I'm just guessing. To me, this is one of the fascinating aspects of beans—once domesticated, they simply evolved through individual efforts. No one took notes. Nonetheless, garboncitos have evolved into a very appealing bean.

Valerie Phipps of Phipps Ranch in Pescadero, California, is the only commercial grower of garboncitos in the United States. She picked up the bean seeds at an outdoor market in Guadalajara, Mexico. She says they look a little like an eastern-grown bean called the China yellow, but they are not botanically the same, although they have similar characteristics.

BEANS

1 cup   dried garboncito beans, soaked and drained
One 3-inch strip   kombu seaweed

TOMATOES

6   large tomatoes
Olive oil spray as needed
Salt, to taste
Crushed red pepper, to taste (optional)
6 cloves   garlic, finely minced
2 tablespoons   minced fresh basil or 2 teaspoons dried basil

TO ASSEMBLE

1 teaspoon   extra virgin olive oil

1 Put the beans in a 3- or 4-quart saucepan. Add the kombu and enough water to cover by 2 inches. Cover, bring to a boil, reduce heat to low, and simmer for 45 to 50 minutes, until the beans are tender yet still hold their shape. Remove and discard the kombu.

2 Meanwhile, preheat oven to 325°F. Cut out the stem of each tomato with a paring knife. Cut the tomatoes in half crosswise. Place, cut-side up, in a ceramic or glass baking dish or on a cookie sheet with sides.

3 Lightly mist each half with olive oil spray. Sprinkle on salt and crushed red pepper, if using. With a bread knife, spread ½ teaspoon of minced garlic over the top of each tomato half. Lightly spray with olive oil again. Bake, uncovered, for 1½ hours.

4 After baking, sprinkle minced basil evenly over the tomato halves, and spray very lightly with more olive oil. Bake for 30 minutes longer. (This can be done in the morning and the tomatoes kept in a cool oven until needed. Right before serving, heat the oven to 325°F again and bake for 5 minutes to heat through.)

5 When beans are done, drain and discard the cooking water and put beans in a mixing bowl. Add the olive oil and stir well.

6 Cut up 8 of the caramelized tomato halves and stir into the beans.

7 Serve the beans topped with a caramelized tomato half or quarter.

Serves 4 to 8

LENTILS WITH MUSHROOMS IN PHYLLO

The day before you want to make this appetizer, take the phyllo dough out of the freezer and put it in the refrigerator overnight. Remove the package from the refrigerator one hour before you want to use the phyllo. Or, if you're like me and you didn't know yesterday what you were going to make today, you can take the dough straight out of the freezer and leave it at room temperature for three to four hours to defrost. Unfortunately, you can't defrost phyllo in the microwave—do not try it! While the phyllo is defrosting, start cooking the lentils and sautéing the mushrooms. It's best if the mixture is cooled before assembling. I always feel "wealthy" when my freezer is stocked with these make-and-freeze appetizers. How impressive to pop a few in the oven when unexpected guests arrive.

Lentils are not technically a bean but a legume, yet they are sometimes called "flat beans." Ninety percent of United States lentils are grown in the Palouse region of Idaho and Washington. They're a favorite of mine because of their deep, strong flavor and their short cooking time. Their added bonus is that you don't need to soak them either.

This appetizer is especially appealing when made with the petite French green lentils (grown in Idaho and Montana), which hold their shape best of all the lentils. Do not use the red lentils, which are decorticated, meaning their outer skin has been removed—they fall apart after ten minutes of cooking. (The red lentils are great for quick soups because they cook in half the time of other lentils.)

1 box (about 20 sheets)	phyllo dough
1 cup	dried lentils
One 3-inch strip	kombu seaweed
½	yellow onion, quartered
2 whole cloves	garlic, peeled
1	carrot, cut into 2-inch chunks
½ pound	shiitake mushrooms
½ pound	cremini mushrooms or white mushrooms
4 cloves	garlic, finely minced
1	yellow onion, diced
2 teaspoons	dried thyme

Pinch	cloves
1 tablespoon	extra virgin olive oil
3 tablespoons	dry red wine
2 teaspoons	low-sodium soy sauce
	Vegetable oil spray as needed
⅔ cup	crumbled feta cheese (optional)

1   Put the lentils in a 3- or 4-quart saucepan. Add the kombu, onion, garlic, carrot, and enough water to cover by 2 inches. Cover, bring to a boil, reduce heat to low, and simmer for 30 to 40 minutes, until the lentils are tender yet still hold their shape. Remove and discard the kombu and vegetables. Set aside.

2   Meanwhile, wipe the mushrooms clean with a damp paper towel. Snip off stems of shiitake mushrooms and discard (or save to flavor a stock). Slice caps. Snap tops of other mushrooms from their stems. Mince the stems and slice the caps.

3   Sauté the mushrooms with the garlic, onion, thyme, and cloves in the olive oil over medium-high heat until the mushrooms become limp. Add red wine when more moisture is needed.

4   Drain lentils and add to sauté pan along with the soy sauce. Reduce heat to medium and cook for 3 to 5 minutes to blend flavors.

5   Place the mushroom/lentil mixture in a bowl and refrigerate. Once cooled, proceed to the next step. (If you assemble when this mixture is warm, the phyllo will become gummy during assembly and less flaky once cooked.)

6   Unwrap the phyllo dough, unfold, and lay out in front of you. Cut the stack of phyllo sheets into six 2-inch-wide strips, 14 inches long, by cutting strips off the short end of the rectangular dough. Stack strips, and cover those you're not using with a damp towel.

7   Take one strip and lightly spray it with vegetable oil spray. Top with another strip and lightly spray again. Add about 1 tablespoon of mushroom/lentil mixture and ½ teaspoon crumbled feta to the edge of the sprayed phyllo strips. Fold phyllo over filling at an angle, making a triangle. Continue to fold the triangle onto itself, spraying lightly with vegetable oil spray after each fold. See illustration on box of phyllo dough.

8 Freeze in a single layer on a cookie sheet, then place in resealable freezer bags and freeze for up to one year. To heat frozen appetizers, bake at 375°F for 15 minutes. To heat unfrozen appetizers, bake right after folding for 10 to 12 minutes. Serve hot or warm.

Makes 60 appetizers

Bean Salads to Start or Make a Meal

BAKED SPINACH AND FETA SALAD WITH SUNFLOWER CUCUMBER DRESSING AND GARBANZO BEAN CROUTONS

Although garbanzo beans grow in the western United States now, they are native to the Middle East. They are an entirely different genus and species of bean, *Cicer arietinum*, than the four types of *Phaseolus* native to the Americas. This import has been thoroughly embraced by Americans, however, and is commonly enjoyed in soups, salads, and dips. Perhaps the best-known use of garbanzo beans is in hummus, a Middle Eastern dip that calls for a purée of cooked garbanzo beans, tahini (sesame seed butter), olive oil, and parsley.

One of my favorite things to do with garbanzo beans is to season and bake them into crunchy nuts, or croutons. Here I add them to a salad of wilted spinach, dressed with a creamy purée of seeds, vegetables, and herbs. The unexpected crunch of the garbanzo croutons makes each bite distinct. This salad is also quite pleasing to the eye: the tops of each individual serving are covered with slices of different-sized tomatoes, while the deep green of the spinach peeks from between the rounds of red.

GARBANZO CROUTONS

One	16-ounce can garbanzo beans, drained and rinsed
1 tablespoon	granulated garlic
1 teaspoon	cayenne
1 teaspoon	low-sodium soy sauce

DRESSING

¼ cup	raw sunflower seeds
One	8-ounce cucumber
2 tablespoons	chopped onion
2 tablespoons	chopped fresh parsley leaves
1 teaspoon	minced fresh thyme leaves
2 tablespoons	apple cider vinegar
3 tablespoons	walnut oil or canola oil

| 2 tablespoons | water |
| Pinch | salt |

SALAD

2 bunches	spinach or 12 ounces spinach leaves
4	medium tomatoes, sliced
16	cherry tomatoes, cut in half lengthwise
¼ cup	feta cheese
1 tablespoon	minced fresh oregano

1   To make the garbanzo bean croutons, first preheat the oven to 350°F. Toss the beans while they're still damp with the garlic, cayenne, and soy sauce. Place on a cookie sheet in a single layer and bake for 60 to 70 minutes, stirring once halfway through. The croutons should be crunchy and lightly browned. Cool and set aside.

2   To make the dressing, put the sunflower seeds in the work bowl of a food processor—make sure the work bowl is dry. Process to a powder.

3   Peel and seed the cucumber and add it, plus the onion, parsley, and thyme, to the food processor. Process, then add the vinegar, oil, water, and salt. Process until creamy, then refrigerate dressing until ready to use.

4   To make the salad, wash the spinach in two changes of water. Discard stems and any discolored leaves. Spin dry.

5   Preheat the oven to Broil.

6   Take out 8 medium-size, shallow, ovenproof dishes (1-inch-deep gratin dishes work well). Pile spinach into each. Add a small handful of garbanzo croutons around the edges of each salad. Pour 2 tablespoons dressing evenly over each salad. Top with sliced tomatoes and halved cherry tomatoes, covering the top of each salad.

7   Divide the feta cheese into 8 equal portions and crumble evenly over the tomatoes. Sprinkle the fresh oregano over the feta.

8   Place the salads under the broiler for 2 to 3 minutes, or until the feta melts and browns lightly and the spinach is slightly wilted. Serve immediately.

Makes 1¼ cups dressing and 8 dinner-size salads

CANNELLINI BEAN SALAD
WITH ROASTED VEGETABLES AND ARUGULA

The cannellini bean, most often associated with Italian cuisine, was originally cultivated in Argentina. It was brought to Italy in the sixteenth century and is still widely grown and eaten there. Its smooth texture and nutlike flavor make it perfect for the Italian flavors of this summer vegetable salad. Although you don't think of the cannellini as an American crop, California's Mediterranean climate is a natural for this ivory-white bean. Italian settlers brought the bean to California in the late 1800s. It is now grown by many boutique bean growers, such as the Phipps Ranch in Pescadero, California.

The cannellini also does well in the altitudes of Santa Fe, New Mexico, where Valerie Phipps' friend and colleague Elizabeth Berry of Gallina Canyon Ranch grows many types of beans and vegetables, especially heirlooms. Phipps and Berry are both passionate about heirloom vegetables! Berry says that heirlooms retain the qualities of their ancestors, which makes them valuable food resources—scientists often turn to heirlooms when trying to breed disease or pest resistance into a food crop. "A single heirloom seed," Berry says, "could hold the key to protecting the future of the world's food supply."

1 cup	dried cannellini beans, soaked and rinsed
One 3-inch piece	kombu seaweed
	Salt, to taste:
2	zucchini (optional)
2	Japanese eggplant (optional)
	Garlic oil spray or other oil spray as needed
4	medium tomatoes, diced
8	green onions, sliced into rounds
12	black olives, preferably Kalamata olives, pits removed, sliced
½ cup	minced fresh basil or 2 tablespoons dried basil
	Black pepper, to taste

2 tablespoons   *mayonnaise*
2 tablespoons   *nonfat plain yogurt*
2 large bunches   *arugula, washed and dried, tough stems removed*
Extra virgin olive oil, if desired

1   Put the beans in a 3- or 4-quart saucepan. Add the kombu and enough water to cover by 2 inches. Cover, bring to a boil, reduce the heat to low, and simmer for 60 minutes, until the beans are tender yet still hold their shape. Remove and discard the kombu. When the beans are done to your liking, taste, season with salt, and set aside.

2   If you are using the zucchini and eggplant, preheat the oven to 350°F. Peel the eggplant and cut lengthwise into ½-inch slices. Slice the zucchini lengthwise into ½-inch slices. Place the slices on a lightly oiled cookie sheet. Spray the tops of the slices lightly with oil, and bake for 15 minutes per side. (Alternatively, on a stovetop or outdoor grill, grill the zucchini and eggplant slices about 10 minutes per side.) Set aside.

3   To assemble the salad, drain the beans and add them, plus the diced tomatoes, green onions, olives, basil, salt, pepper, mayonnaise, and yogurt, to a medium-size mixing bowl. Toss gently to mix.

4   Take out 6 plates. Line the bottoms of the plates with arugula. Mound with the bean mixture and, if using, add the zucchini and eggplant slices around the edges. Serve hot, warm, or cold.

Serves 6

BLACK-EYED PEA AND CHOPPED SUMMER VEGETABLE SALAD WITH CARROT JUICE BASIL DRESSING

I called my best friend, Lynn, who lives in Houston, on New Year's Day, and although in her second month of her third pregnancy and sick as a dog, she was making black-eyed peas. "What do you do with them?" I queried, awaiting a family secret from her husband's fourth-generation Houston household. "I just boil them up once a year," she said. "We all take one bite for good luck and throw them away." I'm certain there's more to the family tradition, but in her condition, one bite was all she could manage. Perhaps she'd eat more at a later date if she tried these!?

Originally from Africa, the black-eyed pea was introduced to Asia three thousand years ago. From there, it came to the United States, where it was grown exclusively in the southeastern part of the country for years. Now, however, California's fresh and dried black-eyed pea production is so large the peas are referred to as California Black Eyes in the industry. With carrot juice in the list of ingredients, this recipe is rather California-ized too.

SALAD

1½ cups	dried black-eyed peas, soaked and drained
One 3-inch piece	kombu seaweed
1	bay leaf
	Salt, to taste
⅔ cup	diced cucumber
⅔ cup	diced red onion
⅔ cup	diced yellow crookneck squash
⅔ cup	diced red bell pepper
1⅓ cups	diced tomato
8 cups	mix of romaine, red leaf, and chard

DRESSING

2 cloves	garlic
One	3- to 4-ounce red bell pepper
One	6-ounce zucchini
½ cup	lightly packed fresh basil leaves
½ cup	fresh carrot juice
¼ cup plus 2 tablespoons	apple cider vinegar
3 tablespoons	extra virgin olive oil
¼ teaspoon	salt
Pinch	cayenne

1 Put the black-eyed peas, kombu, bay leaf, and enough water to cover the peas by 2 inches in a 3- or 4-quart saucepan. Cover, bring to a boil, reduce the heat, and simmer for 40 minutes, or until tender yet still holding their shape. Remove and discard the kombu. Taste the peas, season with salt to taste, and set aside until ready to assemble the salad.

2 Meanwhile, dice all the vegetables and combine in a large mixing bowl.

3 Wash and spin dry the lettuce and chard. Refrigerate the veggies and greens separately until ready to assemble the salad.

4 To make the dressing, put the garlic in the work bowl of a food processor and process until well minced. Chop the red bell pepper and zucchini into chunks and add them to the food processor. Process until very well minced, almost liquified. Add the basil leaves and process until well chopped.

5 Add the remaining ingredients and process until smooth. Refrigerate until ready to assemble the salad.

6 When ready to assemble, toss the greens with about half the Carrot Juice Basil Dressing. Take out 8 salad plates and divide the dressed greens among them. Drain the black-eyed peas and toss them with the chopped veggies. Toss with the remaining half of the dressing. Top the greens with the bean/veggie mixture. Serve immediately.

Makes 8 salads and 2 cups dressing

SPICY ASIAN RICE BEANS WITH MUNG BEAN NOODLES

Rice beans look just like Rice Krispies—a little fatter than a long-grain rice kernel. Their flavor is mild and they have a chewy texture because there is so little soft "insides" to them. They were originally domesticated in Asia centuries ago and, just like other Asian beans (mung beans and soybeans), are now grown in the western United States. Rice beans are grown in limited quantities only because they are not widely known. Make sure to place your order for these beans—they'll surely become one of your favorites.

I've paired them with Asian flavorings, plus mung bean noodles, which are a dried pasta-type noodle, transparent and slightly elastic when cooked. They add to the textural appeal of this dish. Find them in natural food stores or Chinese groceries. If you can't find them, substitute four ounces of udon noodles or spaghetti pasta.

1 cup	dried rice beans, soaked and drained
One 3-inch strip	kombu seaweed
2	red bell peppers
1	jalapeño chile pepper, sliced*
2 teaspoons	minced fresh ginger
1 teaspoon	minced fresh garlic

---

* To slice a chile without touching the parts that can burn you, first cut the tip off the chile. Now you have a flat end on which to stand the chile upright as you slice vertical strips off all around the chile, while holding on to the stem. When done, you'll be holding the stem, with veins and seeds attached (the hot stuff), which you can now discard.

½ teaspoon   crushed red pepper
2 tablespoons   low-sodium soy sauce
3 tablespoons   rice vinegar
1 tablespoon   canola or safflower oil
1 package (2.4 ounces)   mung bean noodles (Harusame), or 4 ounces udon noodles, or 4 ounces spaghetti pasta
2 tablespoons   toasted sesame oil
1 cup   green onions, diagonally sliced
2 tablespoons   black sesame seeds

1   Put the beans in a 3- or 4-quart saucepan. Add the kombu and enough water to cover by 2 inches. Cover, bring to a boil, reduce the heat to low, and simmer for 30 to 35 minutes, until the beans are tender yet still hold their shape. Remove and discard the kombu. Set aside.

2   Preheat the oven to Broil. Bring a pot of water to a boil for the noodles.

3   Roast the red bell peppers as directed in the Basics chapter on page xxii. Slice the peeled peppers into strips and put in a large serving bowl.

4   To make the sauce, combine the sliced jalapeño chile, ginger, garlic, and crushed red pepper in the work bowl of a food processor. Process until the chile is well minced. Add the soy sauce, rice vinegar, and oil. Process to mix and add to the serving bowl.

5   Cook the mung bean noodles in a pot of boiling water for 6 to 8 minutes (or follow package directions for the other noodles). When done, drain the noodles and add to serving bowl.

6   Add the toasted sesame oil, green onions, and black sesame seeds to the serving bowl and toss well.

7   Drain the beans and add to serving bowl. Toss well, then refrigerate, covered, for at least 1 hour to develop flavors.

8   Serve cold.

Serves 6

WHITE TEPARY BEANS AND RICE WITH ZUCCHINI AND PINE NUT DRESSING

Like the Anasazi bean, teparies, which are small flat beans, usually white or golden tan, have the wonderful quality of being less troublesome to our digestive systems than other beans. They were a staple of the Hohokam tribe of Indians who lived near present-day Tucson, Arizona. A thousand years ago, the Hohokam had the most diverse croplands, and thus diet, of any culture living in what is now the United States. Their crops were watered by a vast river-diversion canal system, which at one point was consolidated into a more extensive irrigation system. But drought and other problems came, and many of their crops vanished. Only a few remained, including the tepary bean. It continued to grow successfully in the arid southwest United States for many years. What little rain fell was enough for this drought-resistant bean. Now, since all bean crops are abundantly watered through irrigation, the tepary has become a poor yielder, and is no longer grown commercially.

Tepary beans hold their shape well and taste very mild. This presentation highlights the fresh taste of the dressing and the textural differences between the beans and rice.

BEANS AND RICE

1 cup	dried white tepary beans, soaked and drained
One 3-inch strip	kombu seaweed
	Salt, to taste
2 cups	water
1 cup	basmati rice, rinsed

DRESSING

¼ cup	pine nuts
2 medium (8 ounces total)	zucchini, chopped into 2-inch chunks
1 large clove	garlic
1 cup	loosely packed basil leaves
1 scant teaspoon	lemon zest
3 tablespoons	apple cider vinegar
1 tablespoon	extra virgin olive oil

¼ cup   water
½ teaspoon   salt

SALAD

2 stalks   celery, diced
1   carrot, grated
½   red onion, diced
3   tomatoes, diced
1 head   romaine lettuce, washed and spun dry

1 Put the beans in a 3- or 4-quart saucepan. Add the kombu and enough
water to cover by 2 inches. Cover, bring to a boil, reduce the heat to low,
and simmer for 45 to 60 minutes, until beans are tender yet still hold
their shape. Remove and discard the kombu. Taste the beans, salt to taste,
and set aside.

2 Meanwhile, in a separate pot, bring 2 cups of water to a boil. Slowly add
the rice, cover the pot, bring back to a boil, lower the heat, and simmer
until done, about 30 to 35 minutes. Do not pick up the lid or stir the
rice until it is done.

3 To make the dressing, preheat the oven to 325°F. Put the pine nuts on
a baking sheet or cookie sheet and toast until light golden, about 15
minutes. Let cool.

4 Once cool, put the pine nuts in the dry work bowl of a food processor
and process to a powder.

5 Add the zucchini chunks and process until minced. Scrape down the
sides and process again until it begins to liquify.

6 Add the garlic and basil and process until well minced.

7 Add the remaining dressing ingredients and process until creamy. Refrigerate, covered, until needed. (Dressing can be made up to 2 days in advance.)

8 To assemble the salad, drain the beans. Toss half the salad vegetables
(except lettuce) and half the dressing with the beans, and the other half
of the vegetables and dressing with the rice.

9 Arrange whole romaine leaves on 8 salad plates. Place a scoop of beans
and a scoop of rice on the romaine. Serve warm or cold.

Serves 8

BALBOA ISLAND KIDNEY BEAN TOSTADA SALAD

Kidney beans were introduced to the western United States at the time of the gold rush. They came from Chile, which is why they are sometimes called Chilean beans. They are best adapted to California's growing climate, although a few grow in Nebraska and Michigan. My favorite recipe for kidney beans is this tostada salad, an adaptation of a recipe from my childhood. When I was in grammar school, my friend Patty often invited me to her family's summer home on Balboa Island. Patty's mom made this bean, cheese, and corn chip salad and would serve it to us for lunch. I have to admit I didn't like it then, but I didn't like anything but burgers and chocolate at age nine. When she made it though, its distinct aroma lingered, and I began to associate it with my pleasurable trips to their home. It's a sense memory— like the smell of Coppertone—and such a pleasant one, I wanted to re-create it to again experience the carefree, relaxed days of Balboa. Here is my version of Mrs. Johnson's kidney bean salad, which takes me all the way back to Balboa Island while still sitting in my own kitchen. Wanna come?

½	red onion, diced
1 pound	ground turkey
1 cup	salsa
3 tablespoons	nonfat plain yogurt
One	16-ounce can kidney beans, drained and rinsed
1 small head	romaine lettuce, cut into shreds
6	tomatoes, cut into eighths
	Baked corn chips as needed
½ cup	shredded sharp cheddar cheese

1 Put the onion and turkey in a nonstick skillet and cook over high heat, stirring often, for 3 minutes.
2 Add the salsa, and continue cooking until the turkey is cooked through.
3 Remove to a bowl and stir in the yogurt and beans.
4 Divide romaine lettuce up on 6 plates. Mound equal portions of the turkey and bean salad on top. Surround with tomatoes and corn chips. Top with a sprinkling of cheddar cheese. Serve hot, warm, or cold.

Serves 6

HOPI WOMAN BEAN SALAD

Loretta Barrett Oden of the Corn Dance Cafe in Santa Fe, New Mexico, told me about these big, fat, egg-shaped white beans. They're very much like potatoes, and she prepares them at her restaurant like mashed potatoes. She says that these beans were saved through the generations and passed down from woman to woman, who used them in puberty and fertility rites. First started inside, the sprouted beans were then planted outside when the season was proper, at which point they would spring forth with abundance, bejeweled with showy red flowers.

Below I offer a classic potato salad made with these plump, starchy beans that are also known as pueblo beans, mortgage lifters, and Aztec whites.

1 cup	dried Hopi woman beans, soaked and drained, or large lima beans
One 3-inch strip	kombu seaweed
⅓ cup	red bell pepper, diced
⅓ cup	red onion, diced
⅓ cup	celery, diced
⅓ cup	green onions, sliced
1 clove	garlic, finely minced
2 tablespoons	extra virgin olive oil
1½ tablespoons	apple cider vinegar
1½ tablespoons	Dijon-style mustard
2 tablespoons	nonfat plain yogurt (optional)
1¼ teaspoons	dried dill weed
¾ teaspoon	celery seed
¼ teaspoon	salt

1 Put the beans in a 3- or 4-quart saucepan. Add the kombu and enough water to cover by 2 inches. Cover, bring to a boil, reduce heat to low, and simmer for 60 to 75 minutes, until the beans are tender yet still hold their shape. Remove and discard the kombu.

2 Prepare all vegetables as indicated in the ingredients list and put in a medium-size mixing bowl.

3 In a small bowl, whisk together the olive oil, vinegar, mustard, and yogurt, if using.

4 Add the dill, celery seed, and salt.

5 Drain the beans and combine them with the diced vegetables. Add the olive oil mixture and toss well to combine. Taste and adjust the seasonings. Refrigerate, covered, for 1 hour for flavors to develop further.

Serves 8

BEAN SOUPS

ANASAZI BEAN AND ROASTED CHILE SOUP

Oh, what a story this pretty burgundy bean has! Seems a few years ago an Anasazi bean was found at Mesa Verde, Arizona, near the cliff dwellings of the ancient tribe of Anasazi Indians. (No one knows what these Indians called themselves—*anasazi* is a Navajo word that means "ancient ones.") Although said to be close to eight hundred years old, the story goes, when planted, this bean grew. Most scientists say this is impossible, but perhaps not. Many seeds used to have a coating that protected them from sprouting for many years, such as the locust plant seed, which waited as long as 460 years to pop up in ideal conditions. Nowadays, though, bean seeds have lost that coating, and rely on humans to plant them each year. The Anasazi bean was registered in the late 1980s by Adobe Milling in Dove Creek, Colorado. I can't think of another natural seed with a registered name, but Adobe Milling knew the appeal of a good romantic story when they heard one, and have done a great job popularizing this nutritious bean.

The Anasazi bean is also sold under the names of Aztec bean, cave bean, New Mexico appaloosa, and Jacob's cattle bean. Interestingly enough, the Jacob's cattle bean is known to have been in the Southwest in prehistoric times, but somehow it became a traditional bean of New England.

By whatever name it's known, this widely discussed bean has a sweeter taste than most beans of its size, and it has four times fewer complex sugars of gastric distress fame. It also cooks faster than comparable beans, such as the pinto. And if that isn't enough, it makes a fabulous soup.

2 cups	dried Anasazi beans, soaked and drained
One 6-inch strip	kombu seaweed
1	bay leaf
3 stalks	celery, diced
1	large carrot, sliced
1	large yellow onion, diced
6 cloves	garlic, finely minced
6 cups	fresh water
1	large red bell pepper
3	anaheim (mild), or poblano (hot) chiles

8	whole cloves garlic, skins on
One	15-ounce can diced tomatoes, plus juices
One	12-ounce beer
4 teaspoons	pasilla or ancho chile powder (see Basics chapter, page xxii)
1 teaspoon	ground cumin
½ teaspoon	dried thyme
¼ teaspoon	ground coriander
1 teaspoon	salt
½ teaspoon	black pepper
1 tablespoon	low-sodium soy sauce for garnish
	Chopped fresh cilantro (optional)

1 Put the beans in an 8-quart Dutch oven. Add the kombu, bay leaf, celery, carrot, onion, garlic, and fresh water. Cook for 1 hour and discard the kombu. Cook for 30 to 60 more minutes, or until the beans are tender.

2 Meanwhile, preheat the oven to Broil. Roast the red bell pepper and chiles. (Or use jarred roasted red bells and canned mild green Ortega chiles.) When done, set aside.

3 Roast the garlic as directed in Basics chapter, page xxii. When cool enough to handle, remove and discard the skins from the garlic.

4 Meanwhile, add the tomatoes, plus juices, beer, pasilla or ancho chile powder, cumin, thyme, coriander, salt, black pepper, and soy sauce to the soup. Cook at least 10 minutes longer.

5 Put the peppers/chiles and roasted garlic in the work bowl of a food processor. Add the soup in batches and purée the peppers/chiles/garlic and two-thirds of the soup. Return to the pot and simmer for about 5 minutes more. Taste, and adjust seasonings, if needed. Serve hot, garnished with chopped cilantro.

Serves 10

AUTUMN VEGETABLE BARLEY AND APPALOOSA BEAN SOUP

Appaloosa beans were part of the diet of many Native American tribes. In most native cultures, beans were the responsibility—actually the privilege— of the women to plant, harvest, and cook. It was a sacred rite to sow the beans, and no man was allowed to touch them. Beans are actually dormant embryos, as the seeds in a woman's ovaries were viewed, and so were considered very mystical phenomena, the domain of women.

1 cup	dried appaloosa beans, soaked and drained
6 cups	Garden-Fresh Vegetable Stock (see following recipe), or chicken broth
One 3-inch piece	kombu seaweed
6 cloves	garlic, finely minced
1 tablespoon	extra virgin olive oil
1½ cups	diced unpeeled potatoes, about 1 large potato
1½ cups	diced unpeeled yams, about 1 medium yam
2 stalks	celery, diced
1	carrot, sliced
2 cups	sliced leeks, white and pale green parts only, about 2 large leeks
2 tablespoons	dried barley
3 cups	chopped greens (chard or spinach or escarole)
1	medium tomato, chopped
1 teaspoon	dried basil
¼ teaspoon	dried summer savory
¼ teaspoon	dried marjoram
⅛ teaspoon	dried rosemary
2 teaspoons	low-sodium soy sauce
	Salt, to taste

1 Put the beans in an 8-quart Dutch oven. Add the vegetable stock or chicken broth and kombu. Cover, bring to a boil, reduce the heat to low, and simmer for 40 minutes.

2 Meanwhile, in a large sauté pan, sauté the garlic in the olive oil over low heat until the garlic turns a light golden color, about 5 minutes.

3 Add the potatoes, yams, celery, carrots, leeks, and barley to the sauté pan. Cook over high heat for 2 minutes, stirring constantly to coat vegetables with the oil. Add the contents of the sauté pan to the pot of beans. Bring to a boil, turn the heat to low, cover the pan, and simmer for 30 minutes. After 30 minutes, remove and discard the kombu.

4 When the beans are tender, purée 2 ladlesful of the soup in a food processor or blender, then return the mixture to the soup pot.

5 Add the chopped greens, tomato, herbs, and soy sauce. Let simmer for at least 15 minutes longer.

6 Taste. Since the vegetable stock is unsalted, you may want to add more soy sauce or salt to taste. Serve immediately.

Serves 8

GARDEN-FRESH VEGETABLE STOCK

8 cups	cold water
2 cloves	garlic, crushed
1	yellow onion, diced
1	carrot, sliced into rounds
1 stalk	celery, diced
1	leek, chopped
2 medium or 1 large	tomato, chopped
10 to 15	stems plus leaves of parsley
One 4-inch piece	fresh rosemary, or 1 teaspoon dried rosemary
2	bay leaves
Six	4-inch stems plus leaves of fresh thyme, or ½ teaspoon dried thyme
1 teaspoon	black peppercorns
2	whole cloves (optional)
One 3-inch piece	kombu seaweed (optional)

1 Put all the ingredients in a stockpot, cover with water, bring to a boil, turn the heat to low, and simmer for 1 hour.
2 Remove and discard the vegetables.
3 Store stock, covered, in the refrigerator for up to 1 week, or freeze for up to 4 months.

Makes 1 quart unsalted vegetable stock

SNOWCAP BEAN AND EGGPLANT SOUP

Snowcap beans are a tan bean with a "snowcap" of white along the side, and random spots of burgundy speckling overall. I think it is one of the most beautiful of all the beans in this book. Although I know it is an oddball, found in a crop of some other bean, I can't help but wonder if it is a throwback to a bean that existed during the time of the Incas, who used beans as a means of communication. Apparently, beans of different colors, sizes, and shapes were each given a meaning. Runners would carry them and their important messages long distances from one leader to another. A handful of beans held a world of information, which was deciphered by a cryptographer, who would then announce the news of the day. Was there a bean then that looked like the snowcap? What was its unique meaning?

2 cups	dried snowcap beans, soaked and drained
7 cups	water
1	bay leaf
One 6-inch strip	kombu seaweed
1	large eggplant, about 1½ pounds
	Vegetable oil spray
6 cloves	garlic, finely minced
1	red onion, diced
1 teaspoon	dried basil
½ teaspoon	dried oregano
¼ teaspoon	dried thyme
⅛ teaspoon	dried rosemary
⅛ teaspoon	dried sage
⅛ teaspoon	fennel seeds
½ teaspoon	crushed red pepper flakes
2 tablespoons	extra virgin olive oil
2 pounds	fresh tomatoes, peeled and seeded (see Basics chapter, page xxii), or one 28-ounce can whole tomatoes, drained of juices
1 teaspoon	salt
½ teaspoon	black pepper
1 tablespoon	low-sodium soy sauce

1 Put the beans in an 8-quart Dutch oven. Add fresh water, bay leaf, and kombu. Cover, bring to a boil, reduce heat, and simmer for 1 hour. Remove and discard the kombu. Cook for 30 to 60 more minutes, or until the beans are tender.

2 Preheat the oven to 350°F. Peel and slice the eggplant into 1-inch slices, and place on a lightly oiled cookie sheet. Lightly spray the tops of the eggplant slices with oil, and bake for 20 minutes. Remove from the oven, dice, and set aside.

3 In a sauté pan, sauté the garlic, onion, herbs, fennel seeds, and crushed red pepper in the olive oil over medium heat until the onion is transparent, 5 to 10 minutes.

4 When the beans are tender, add the sautéed mixture. Add the tomatoes, salt, pepper, and soy sauce.

5 Purée two-thirds of the soup, then add the reserved eggplant. Simmer 15 minutes, then serve hot.

Serves 8 to 10

LIMA BEAN AND ESCAROLE SOUP WITH HERBED TOMATO SALSA

The lima bean was originally grown in Central America in—guess where—Lima, Peru, where it was dated at five thousand years old. It came to the United States in the early nineteenth century. In a study called *Vegetables of New York*, by U. P. Hedrick, it was reported that in 1824 Captain John Harris of the U.S. Navy brought the lima bean seed from Lima and grew it on his farm in Chester, New York. By the late 1840s, lima beans were being shipped directly from Peru to California for the gold miners to eat. It is probably at this time that the lima bean got its current name, a mispronunciation of Lima, their port of origin. Because of similarities in climate, 100 percent of the American production of large lima beans is now in California.

This aromatic soup is simmered with a piece of cheese rind, which lends the broth its lovely perfume and flavor, with very little added fat. This particular cheese, Reggiano Parmigiano, is the original Parmesan cheese. It's expensive, and suitably so for its rich, nutlike flavor. Even though the cheese is worth its heady price, you'll be happy to know what to do with its twelve-dollar-per-pound rind—plop it right into this pot of soup! The finished soup is topped with a lightly cooked salsa, richly flavored with herbs, garlic, and vinegar. Although it's said that limas are one of the most difficult beans to digest, never fear with this recipe! Besides soaking the beans, then cooking them with kombu, add miso for a dose of beneficial bacteria to aid digestion. The vinegar in the salsa helps break down the complex sugars in the beans before they become a problem, and the greens add potassium to stimulate your gastric juices. All this chemistry, and a good bowl of soup, at that. This is the best a lima bean can be.

SOUP

2 cups	dry small or large lima beans, soaked and drained
9 cups	water
One 6-inch piece	kombu seaweed
2	bay leaves
2 x 3-inch rind	Reggiano Parmigiano (optional)

2	leeks, white parts only, sliced
6 cloves	garlic, finely minced
1	carrot, diced
1¼ teaspoons	dried basil
¼ teaspoon	dried rosemary
4 cups	escarole or romaine, washed and chopped
2 tablespoons	mellow white, or mellow yellow miso
	Salt, to taste
	Black pepper, to taste

SALSA

2 pounds	tomatoes, peeled and seeded (see Basics chapter, page xxii)
1 teaspoon	dried basil
2 cloves	garlic, finely minced
¼ cup	minced fresh parsley
¼ teaspoon	cayenne
2 teaspoons	extra virgin olive oil
1 tablespoon plus 1 teaspoon	red wine vinegar
	Salt, to taste
	Black pepper, to taste

1 Put the beans in an 8-quart Dutch oven. Add fresh water, kombu, bay leaves, rind of cheese, if using, sliced leeks, garlic, and diced carrots. Cover, bring to a boil, reduce the heat, and simmer for 1 hour. Remove the kombu and cook 15 to 30 minutes more, or until beans are tender.

2 Remove the cheese rind and bay leaves. Purée one-third of the soup. Return to the pot.

3 Add the basil, rosemary, and escarole or romaine. Cook, covered, for 15 minutes. Add more water, if needed, about ½ to 1 cup.

4 Right before serving, mix the miso with a cup or so of hot broth. Stir to mix well, then return mixture to pot of soup. Taste and season soup with salt and pepper, if needed.

5 Meanwhile, to make the salsa, first peel and seed the tomatoes. Dice the tomatoes.

6 Put the tomatoes, dried basil, and garlic in a large nonstick skillet. Turn the heat to high and cook for 2 minutes, stirring occasionally.

7 Remove from the heat and stir in the parsley, cayenne, olive oil, and vinegar. Add salt and pepper to taste, if needed.

8 To serve, ladle out the soup into bowls. Top with about ¼ cup Herbed Tomato Salsa per bowl and serve, or serve the salsa alongside in a small bowl to be added to the soup at the table.

Serves 10

BUCKSKIN BEAN SOUP, WESTERN-STYLE

The buckskin bean is an heirloom bean from Oregon, now grown by a few boutique bean growers for mail-order purchase. It has a real cowboy taste to it, so it can take aggressive flavors, as presented here.

1 cup	dried buckskin beans, soaked and rinsed, or lentils
One 3-inch strip	kombu seaweed
1½ stalks	celery, diced
1	small carrot, sliced or diced
1 pound	fresh tomatoes, or one 15-ounce can tomatoes (omit step #2)
½	large red onion, diced
2 cloves	garlic, minced
2 teaspoons	ground cumin
1 teaspoon	dried oregano
¾ teaspoon	ground coriander
¼ teaspoon	cayenne
1 tablespoon	extra virgin olive oil
2 tablespoons	low-sodium soy sauce

1 Put the beans in a 3- or 4-quart saucepan. Add the kombu, celery, carrots, and enough water to cover by 2 inches. Cover, bring to a boil, reduce the heat to low, and simmer for 60 minutes, until the beans are tender. Remove and discard the kombu.

2 Meanwhile, preheat the oven to Broil. If using fresh tomatoes, cut out the stems, then cut the tomatoes in half crosswise. Place the tomato halves cut-side down on a cookie sheet and broil for 8 to 9 minutes, or until the skins pop up. Remove from the oven and set aside.

3 In a sauté pan, sauté the onion, garlic, and spices over medium heat in the olive oil until the onion is transparent, about 5 minutes.

4 When the beans are tender, add the sautéed mixture to the pot.

5 Remove and discard the skin from the tomatoes. With a pair of cook's tongs, squeeze the seeds out of the tomatoes and add the tomatoes, which should be very soft, to the pot of soup.

6 Purée half the soup in a food processor or blender. (If using lentils, no need to purée half the soup.) Add soy sauce, taste, and adjust seasonings. Simmer 5 minutes more to blend flavors, then serve hot.

Serves 6

WHITE BEAN AND ZUCCHINI "CREAM" SOUP WITH BROKEN PASTA

Native Americans were very talented at cultivating different varieties and colors of beans and corn. Through crossing and selection, they created six colors of beans to symbolize the four cardinal points on a compass, plus two other directions. White beans signified the east, while blue beans, such as the blue-black Mitla bean, indicated west. Red beans were for south, and yellow, north. Multicolored or mottled beans were created for zenith, or up, and black indicated nadir, or down.

The original small white bean was obtained from Indians of New York State sometime before the end of the nineteenth century, but is lost to us now. What we eat today is a distant relative. In this white bean soup, the "cream" is really a purée of sautéed vegetables and fresh herbs that is stirred into the finished soup, adding body and loads of fresh, summery flavor.

SOUP

1½ cups	dried small white beans, or navy beans, soaked and drained
6 cups	low- or no-sodium chicken broth or vegetable broth
One 6-inch strip	kombu seaweed (optional)
2	bay leaves
One	16-ounce can whole tomatoes plus juices, or 1 pound fresh tomatoes, peeled and seeded (see Basics chapter, page xxii)
½ teaspoon	dried thyme
1 teaspoon	salt
¼ cup	pasta (any shape, broken into bite-size pieces—try lasagna noodles or the thick perciatelli noodles)

ZUCCHINI CREAM

1 tablespoon	extra virgin olive oil
6 cloves	garlic, finely minced

½ teaspoon	crushed red pepper
1	medium yellow onion, diced
1	medium carrot, sliced
3 (1 pound total)	zucchini, sliced
½ cup	loosely packed fresh parsley leaves
1 cup	loosely packed fresh basil leaves

1 Put the beans in an 8-quart Dutch oven. Add the chicken broth, kombu, and bay leaves. Cover, bring to a boil, reduce the heat to low, and simmer for 45 to 60 minutes, until the beans are tender. Remove and discard the kombu.

2 Once the beans are tender, add the canned tomatoes, crushing them with your fingers as you add them to the pot, plus the juices, or fresh tomatoes, dried thyme, salt, and broken pasta pieces. Cover and continue to cook for at least 10 minutes to ensure the pasta is tender.

3 Meanwhile, put the olive oil, garlic, and crushed red pepper in a large sauté pan and sauté over low heat until the garlic turns light golden, about 10 minutes.

4 Add the onion, carrots, and zucchini to the sauté pan. Raise the heat to high. Toss the vegetables well to coat with the oil, garlic, and peppers. Cover, lower the heat to medium, and cook for 10 minutes. If needed, add a touch of water to the pan to ensure the vegetables steam and don't burn. Cook until the vegetables are tender.

5 Meanwhile, put the parsley and basil leaves in the work bowl of a food processor. Process until well minced.

6 Add the vegetables in the sauté pan to the food processor and process until well puréed, making a zucchini "cream."

7 Add the zucchini cream to the pot of soup. Stir well, then serve immediately.

Serves 8

BUTTERSCOTCH CALYPSO BEAN AND SPAGHETTI SQUASH SOUP

Rumor has it that this yellow and white bean is the original Boston baked bean. When the settlers found the grain they'd brought from the Old World didn't grow here, the native peoples in the Northeast showed them how to bake these beans, also known as Yellow Eye beans. Put the beans in a clay vessel, add a little maple syrup, wild onions, and water. Bury in a fire pit for two to three days, the original recipe continues, and slowly simmer until soft and sweet.

Marked like the black and white calypso beans with a distinctive yin-yang symbol, butterscotch calypsos are now grown in Idaho and New Mexico. As this soup demonstrates, there's much more you can do with butterscotch calypso beans than baking them with sugar, although a certain sweetness does complement their flavor. I've found that a sweetener, such as maple syrup, eaten with beans upsets digestion, so I use herbs and vegetables for sweetness instead. Basil, tarragon, onion, carrots, tomatoes, and spaghetti squash offer sweetness and more layers of flavor than maple syrup does, as well as better nutrition.

Spaghetti squash can be used in place of pasta or noodles in many recipes. When you do so, you gain the extra fiber and nutrients that this beta-carotene-rich winter squash has to offer. I once suggested to a student of mine that she toss spaghetti squash with her favorite tomato sauce. I could sense her hesitancy when I said this. It turns out she thought that all winter squash tasted like pumpkin. Absolutely not the case with this yellow watermelon-shaped squash. Its pale golden spaghettilike strands taste very mild—almost bland—allowing them to blend in anywhere.

2 cups	dried butterscotch calypso beans, soaked and drained
One 6-inch strip	kombu seaweed
3 stalks	celery, sliced
1	large yellow onion, diced
1 small (2 to 2½ pounds)	spaghetti squash

6 cloves	garlic, finely minced
1 tablespoon	extra virgin olive oil
1 teaspoon	dried basil
½ teaspoon	dried thyme
½ teaspoon	dried tarragon
1 teaspoon	salt
¼ teaspoon	black pepper
One	16-ounce can tomatoes, plus juices
2	carrots, grated
1 cup	shredded fresh basil or parsley

1 Put the beans in an 8-quart Dutch oven. Add the kombu, celery, onion, and enough water to cover by 2 inches. Cover, bring to a boil, reduce the heat to low, and simmer for 45 to 60 minutes, until the beans are tender. Remove and discard the kombu.

2 Meanwhile, preheat the oven to 350°F. Poke a few holes in the whole spaghetti squash. Place in the oven and bake for 1 to 1½ hours, or until tender.

3 When the squash is done and has cooled enough to handle, cut it in half lengthwise, scrape away and discard the seeds and strings. With a fork, scrape out the flesh, which will come out in spaghettilike strands, to equal 4 cups. (If you have surplus squash, serve with a favorite spaghetti sauce, or simply with a dusting of Reggiano Parmigiano cheese.)

4 In a small skillet, sauté the garlic in olive oil over low heat until the garlic turns light golden, about 10 minutes.

5 Add the herbs, salt, and pepper to the sauté pan and cook 2 minutes. Add the garlic mixture to the beans once the beans are tender.

6 Add the tomatoes and spaghetti squash and cook 10 minutes.

7 Add the grated carrots and shredded basil. Stir, and serve immediately.

Serves 8

INDIAN WOMAN YELLOW BEAN SOUP WITH MUSHROOMS AND SPINACH

Indian Woman yellow beans were grown by the Native Americans in Montana. They look and taste very much like buckskin beans, yet they are different plants. The Indian Woman yellow bean matures earlier in the season than buckskins, indicative of its northern roots, where it has to come to maturity earlier as the growing season is shorter. With such an evocative name, there must be a story, but much to my frustration, I can't find it. Which reminds me of a story I do have, but not the bean it relates to! There was a man named Burt Berrier, a John Deere farm machinery demonstrator, who collected beans for thirty years while working his way throughout the small towns of the West. He collected the beans that Brigham Young reputedly carried with him from the Midwest to Utah. A native Southwestern bean was given to him by a Navajo woman who, the story goes, was only able to grow it by hauling pots of water across miles of desert. It wasn't the Indian Woman yellow bean—they had different climatic requirements—but it sure must have been tasty for that woman to haul water across a scorching desert to keep it growing.

2 cups	dried Indian Woman yellow or buckskin beans, soaked and drained, or lentils
8 cups	water
One 6-inch strip	kombu seaweed
1	bay leaf
3 stalks	celery, sliced
2	carrots, sliced into rounds
1	red onion, diced
10	shiitake mushrooms, approximately 3 ounces
6 cloves	garlic, finely minced
1/8 to 1/4 teaspoon	cayenne
1 teaspoon	dried basil
1/4 teaspoon	dried thyme
1/4 teaspoon	dried sage

1 tablespoon	extra virgin olive oil
1 teaspoon	salt
1 tablespoon	low-sodium soy sauce
4 cups	spinach leaves

1   Put the beans in an 8-quart Dutch oven. Add fresh water, kombu, bay leaf, celery, carrots, and onion. Cover, bring to a boil, reduce the heat to low, and simmer for 60 to 90 minutes, until the beans are tender. Remove and discard the kombu and bay leaf.

2   Meanwhile, wipe the shiitake mushrooms with a damp paper towel to remove any dirt. Snip off and discard the stems and slice the caps. (The stems can be saved for stock. See Mushroom Vegetable Stock, page 78.)

3   Put the shiitake mushrooms, garlic, spices, and olive oil in a sauté pan and sauté over medium heat until the mushrooms are limp, about 5 minutes.

4   When the beans are tender, purée a few ladlesful (no need to purée if substituting lentils), then add the sauté mixture, plus the salt, soy sauce, and spinach leaves. Cover and cook 5 to 10 minutes more, until the spinach leaves have wilted. Serve immediately.

Serves 8

APPALOOSA BEAN CHILI WITH CHIPOTLE CHILES

Black and white spotted appaloosa beans take their name from their markings, which look remarkably like Appaloosa horses. Frankly, they look a lot like dalmatians too, so it tells you a little about the world when those beans were named: no pedigreed dogs in the eighteenth-century West! There are also some red and white beans sold as red New Mexico appaloosa beans, which I have a sneaking suspicion are the same as Anasazi beans. There are also beans named simply "appaloosa," which are smaller and marked differently—white with dark brown and tan markings at one end only. Use any of the appaloosas for this recipe, as they have similar tastes, although take note that the larger beans will take about fifteen minutes longer to cook. You'll find appaloosas have a cleaner note to them than pintos, and are not as starchy and gummy.

Chipotle chiles are dried and smoked jalapeño chiles. You can find them dried in packages, but they are most commonly found in a can, either alone, or smothered in a tomato sauce called "adobo sauce," which I call for here. They are extremely hot, so I suggest you remove some, if not all, of the seeds, which carry most of the heat. The chiles' predominant taste is smoky, so they lend a barbecue flavor to this simple-to-prepare chili. Chipotle chiles are a worthwhile staple for any pantry, as they can be added to everything from soup to eggs. Once opened, transfer them to a glass jar and store, covered, in the refrigerator indefinitely.

2 cups	dried appaloosa beans, soaked and drained
8 cups	water
One 6-inch strip	kombu seaweed
1	bay leaf
2 stalks	celery, sliced
2	carrots, sliced
1	yellow onion, diced
6 cloves	garlic, finely minced
3	canned chipotle chiles, seeded and minced, plus 1 tablespoon adobo sauce

1 tablespoon	extra virgin olive oil
2 teaspoons	ground cumin
2 teaspoons	chili powder
1 teaspoon	dried oregano
1 teaspoon	salt
One	28-ounce can whole tomatoes, plus juices
1	ear of corn, husked and kernels cut off, or 1 cup frozen corn, rinsed to defrost
½ cup	chopped fresh cilantro for garnish

1   Put the beans in an 8-quart Dutch oven. Add fresh water, kombu, and bay leaf. Cover, bring to a boil, reduce the heat to low, and simmer for 60 minutes, until the beans are tender. Remove and discard the kombu and bay leaf.

2   Meanwhile, sauté the celery, carrot, onion, garlic, and chipotle chiles, plus adobo sauce, in the olive oil over medium heat until the onion is transparent, about 5 minutes. Add the spices and cook for 2 to 3 minutes more, stirring well to distribute the spices among the vegetables.

3   Once the beans are tender, add the sautéed mixture plus the canned tomatoes and their juices, crushing them as you add them to the pot. Return to a boil, cover, lower the heat, and simmer for 10 minutes.

4   Pureé half of the soup in a food processor or blender.

5   Add the corn, heat through, then serve with fresh cilantro sprinkled on the top of each bowl of chili.

Serves 8 to 10

RATTLESNAKE BEAN POTAGE FOR AUTUMN

Rattlesnake beans derive their arresting name from the way their pods twist and turn on themselves as they grow longer—just like a coiled snake. I tend to like smaller beans, so I often use these more diminutive beans when a recipe calls for pintos, a larger, meatier bean with a similar taste.

The "three sisters"—beans, squash, and corn—are in this soup. Native Americans traditionally planted these three vegetables together. As the corn grows, the bean vine coils up its stalk. The squash is planted at the base, where its broad leaves hold in the moisture and smother any weeds. They not only grow cooperatively, but this Indian triad is also complementary in taste and texture when cooked together.

Because this soup takes a little advance preparation, it is perfect for a weekend day when you're doing other chores around the house. Soak the beans, defrost the stock, bake the squash, and make the roasted tomato purée hours before you put the soup on. It's then a very simple proposition to finish it off. The aromas from each step will tantalize all day long.

2 cups	dried rattlesnake beans, soaked and drained
One 6-inch strip	kombu seaweed
1	bay leaf
6 cloves	garlic, finely minced
1	large yellow onion, diced
3 stalks	celery, diced
8 cups	Homemade Chicken Stock (see page 56)
2 cups (about 1 pound)	kabocha squash, or butternut squash
¾ cup	roasted tomato purée (see Basics chapter, page xxiii), or canned tomato purée
2	red, yellow, or orange bell peppers, diced
1 teaspoon	salt
1 teaspoon	dried basil
½ teaspoon	dried thyme
1 tablespoon	low-sodium soy sauce
8 cups	chopped chard leaves, about 6 large leaves
½ cup	fresh or frozen corn kernels

1   Preheat the oven to 350°F.

2   Put the beans in an 8-quart Dutch oven. Add the kombu, bay leaf, garlic, onion, celery, and Homemade Chicken Stock. Cover, bring to a boil, reduce the heat to low, and simmer for 60 minutes, until the beans are tender. Remove and discard the kombu and bay leaf.

3   Meanwhile, poke 2 knife holes in the whole squash and place in the oven. Place a pan with water underneath the rack the squash is on to catch any drips. Bake for 30 minutes, or until just tender (it will not be completely baked at this point). Remove from the oven and when cool enough to handle, cut in half, remove and discard the seeds and strings, peel, and dice 2 cups. Set aside. (Use the remaining squash for vegetable sautés or mash with a little fresh ginger.)

4   Once the beans are tender, add the squash, roasted or canned tomato purée, bell peppers, salt, spices, and soy sauce. Cook for 30 minutes longer to blend flavors. Purée one-third of the soup in a food processor. Return to the pot and continue to simmer.

5   Fifteen minutes before serving, add the chard leaves and cook until wilted. Taste the soup, adjust the seasonings, and add the corn 5 minutes before serving.

Serves 8

HOMEMADE CHICKEN STOCK

3 pounds	chicken bones (backs, necks, wings)
16 cups	water
2	medium yellow onions, chopped
2	medium carrots, sliced into rounds
2 stalks	celery, sliced
4 cloves	garlic, crushed
3 sprigs	fresh thyme or ¼ teaspoon dried thyme
6 sprigs	fresh parsley
¼ teaspoon	black peppercorns
1	bay leaf

1 Place all the ingredients into an 8-quart stockpot. Bring to a boil, reduce the heat to low, cover, and simmer for 2 hours. Skim off the foam periodically.

2 Strain the vegetables and bones through a strainer or colander, and discard. Refrigerate the broth, covered, for 8 hours, or overnight. The fat will rise to the surface and harden, allowing you to spoon it off easily. Use within 2 days, or freeze for up to 3 months.

Makes 16 cups (twice as much as needed for Rattlesnake Bean Potage, so use half and freeze the rest)

STOVETOP BEAN MAIN DISHES

SMALL WHITE BEANS AND FRESH ARTICHOKES WITH LIGHT LEMON DILL VINAIGRETTE

The small white bean, member of the *Phaseolus vulgaris* common bean family, was specifically adapted to the growing conditions of the moist California coast. Up until the late 1980s, thousands of acres were planted in the small white bean, grown mostly for the large canned Boston baked bean market. This location, however, is also the ideal climate for high-profit vegetables such as broccoli, cauliflower, and lettuce. The poor small white bean—doesn't it sound pale, tiny, and helpless?—couldn't compete. It's now grown in the less expensive fields of Idaho, Colorado, Kansas, and Washington. By the way, the difference between the small white bean and navy beans, often used interchangeably in recipes, is that the navy bean is an eastern pea bean, a little larger and rounder than the small white. Either bean, paired here with the artichokes of Castroville, California, is mild enough in flavor to showcase the subtle richness of the artichoke heart.

BEANS

2 cups	dried small white or navy beans, soaked and drained
One 6-inch strip	kombu seaweed
1	bay leaf
2 cloves	garlic, sliced

ARTICHOKES

4	large artichokes
5 to 6 cups	water
1	bay leaf
	Juice from 1 lemon

VINAIGRETTE

3 tablespoons	fresh lemon juice
2 tablespoons	extra virgin olive oil
2 tablespoons	minced fresh dill, or 2 teaspoons dried dill weed
	Salt, to taste
	Black pepper, to taste

TO FINISH

4 cloves	garlic, finely minced
¼ to ½ teaspoon	crushed red pepper
2 tablespoons	extra virgin olive oil

1 Put the beans in a 3- or 4-quart saucepan. Add the kombu, bay leaf, sliced garlic, and enough water to cover by 2 inches. Cover, bring to a boil, reduce the heat to low, and simmer for 40 minutes (the beans will not be completely done). Remove and discard the kombu and bay leaf. Drain the beans, reserving 1¼ cups of the cooking water. (You may now cover and refrigerate the beans and the water and finish cooking them later that day or the next day.)

2 To prepare the artichokes, cut the stems off of each. Using a serrated bread knife, cut off the top 25 percent of the artichoke leaves. With kitchen shears, cut off the remaining pointed tips of the leaves.

3 Place the artichokes in a wide, shallow pan, preferably an 8-quart Dutch oven. Add the water, bay leaf, and juice from 1 lemon. Bring to a boil, turn the heat to low, and simmer for 45 to 50 minutes.

4 When done, remove from the pan and let cool until you can handle them. Remove all the leaves and reserve them in a large mixing bowl. Scrape the choke away from the heart, discard the choke, and chop the hearts into 1½-inch pieces and put in a shallow bowl.

5 Combine the vinaigrette ingredients and pour over the chopped artichoke hearts. Let marinate for at least 30 minutes, but up to a couple days is fine if covered and refrigerated. Stir occasionally.

6 When ready to finish the dish, in a large sauté pan, cook the garlic and crushed red pepper in the olive oil over low heat until they just start to sizzle, about 5 minutes. Add the beans and toss well to coat with oil and flavorings. Now add about 1 cup of the reserved bean water, bring to a boil, turn the heat to low and simmer, uncovered, for 25 minutes, stirring occasionally. If the mixture needs more water during the 25 minutes of cooking, use the remaining ¼ cup of reserved bean water. If not, discard.

7 When done, remove from the heat and add the artichoke hearts and vinaigrette to the beans. Toss well. Taste and adjust the seasonings, adding more salt, black pepper, or lemon juice if needed.

8 To serve, spoon the beans onto plates. Surround with reserved artichoke leaves. Serve hot, warm, or at room temperature.

Serves 8

BLACK TURTLE BEAN PATTIES WITH FRESH SQUASH SALSA

I was truly amazed to find that the black bean was not widely grown in California, because it's certainly widely eaten here. There is a variety, BTS 39, bred by the University of California for California's particular growing conditions, but other varieties of black beans are grown in New Mexico, Michigan, New York, and most notably, in other Western countries such as Mexico and those in Central and South America. I think it is because we have so many natives of these countries in California that the black bean seems indigenous to our young culture. It is also the bean associated with Southwest cuisine, and for my money, it is one of the most flavorful of all beans. I discovered that the tannins that carry color also carry flavor—the more pigment, the more taste. Color also conveys disease resistance—the color compounds, or phenolics, don't suit bug taste buds.

You can make these patties, then cover and refrigerate them up to two days before cooking. They're also great between a hamburger bun with all the usual fixings.

BEAN PATTIES

1 cup	dried black beans, soaked and drained
One 3-inch strip	kombu seaweed
1 tablespoon	low-sodium soy sauce
½	yellow onion, diced
2 cloves	garlic, finely minced
2 tablespoons	cornmeal
½ teaspoon	salt
½ teaspoon	black pepper
½ teaspoon	ground cumin
6 tablespoons	diced canned green chiles (one 4-ounce can)
1	egg, lightly beaten
	Vegetable oil spray as needed

TO FINISH

1 cup Yogurt Cheese (see Basics chapter, page xxiii)

SALSA

1 clove garlic, finely minced
½ red onion, finely diced
¼ red bell pepper, finely diced
1 zucchini, finely diced
1 yellow crookneck squash, finely diced
2 tablespoons minced fresh cilantro
1 tomato, peeled and seeded (see Basics chapter, page xxii)

1 Put the beans in a 3- or 4-quart saucepan. Add the kombu and enough water to cover by 2 inches. Cover, bring to a boil, reduce the heat to low, and simmer for 45 to 60 minutes, until the beans are tender. Remove and discard the kombu.

2 Drain the beans and put in a medium-size mixing bowl. Mash with a fork until most of the beans are broken up.

3 Add the soy sauce, onion, garlic, cornmeal, salt, black pepper, cumin, chiles, and egg. Stir well to mix.

4 Form into 8 to 10 patties. Place on a plate lined with waxed paper to prevent sticking, and if you have the time, refrigerate them.

5 When ready to cook, spray a nonstick skillet with vegetable oil spray and heat. Add the patties and cook until golden, 3 to 5 minutes on each side.

6 To make the salsa, combine all the ingredients in a small mixing bowl. Purée ¼ cup of the mixture, then stir back into the salsa.

7 To serve, top the patties with salsa and a dollop of Yogurt Cheese. These patties are also good with Avocado Cream, Green Chile Sauce (see recipes, pages 70 and 75), and your favorite salsa.

Serves 8 to 10

VEGETARIAN BLACK BEAN AND CONFETTI TAMALES

There is a black bean called the Mitla, now grown in northern New Mexico, that originated in the Mitla Valley in Oaxaca, Mexico. It is not as round as the black turtle bean, and its leaf shape and growing characteristics lead some agriculturists to think it might be a member of the tepary bean family. When you cook the Mitla, it makes a lovely broth, as do the teparies. A church worker in Oaxaca reports that the local women use the broth from this bean to dye their *rebounceas*, or shawls. They come out a blue-black color, like ink.

I was unsuccessful in finding any of these beans during the writing of this book, but they might be available now; check the latest mail-order catalog (see "Sources for Beans and Seeds," page 91). You can use them, or black turtle beans, to make these tamales. If you like, make a double batch of the tamales and freeze them, uncooked. When ready to cook, pop them right in the steamer pot, no defrosting necessary, but steam them fifteen minutes longer than called for in the recipe below.

TAMALE DOUGH

2½ cups	fresh corn kernels, or frozen and defrosted
¾ teaspoon	salt
1 teaspoon	baking powder
2½ cups	corn flour (masa harina)
2 teaspoons	ground cumin
½ cup	chopped fresh cilantro
½ cup	chopped fresh parsley
½ cup	canola oil
¼ cup	water
40 to 50	corn husks

CONFETTI FILLING

One	16-ounce can black beans, rinsed
4 cloves	garlic, finely minced
¼	red bell pepper, finely diced
¼	yellow bell pepper, finely diced
2	scallions, sliced into rounds
½ to ¾ cup	crumbled feta cheese

1 To make tamale dough, put the corn kernels, salt, and baking powder in a food processor and process into a chunky purée. Add the corn flour, cumin, cilantro, and parsley. Pulse until well mixed. Add the oil. Pulse to mix. Add the water and process into a moist dough. Let sit for 15 minutes.

2 Meanwhile, bring a large pot of water to a boil. Put in the corn husks and boil for 5 minutes. Drain well and set aside.

3 Prepare the filling ingredients. Toss together the black beans, garlic, bell peppers, and scallion rounds. Set aside.

4 To assemble the tamales, flatten and overlap two husks on a work surface, points at same end.

5 Use approximately ¼ cup dough and press into a 4 x 5-inch rectangle.

6 Spoon about 2 tablespoons bean/confetti filling down the center. Sprinkle a small amount of feta cheese over this, about 1 teaspoon.

7 Using the husks as your guide, press the tamale dough over to enclose the filling. Roll the husks up, enclosing the tamale dough completely. Twist one end and tie with a strip of corn husk, or jute string. Twist the other end and tie the same way. Continue to assemble the remaining tamales in the same manner.

8 Place the tamales in 2 stacking steamer baskets (or steam them in batches). Bring the water to a boil, add steamer baskets, and steam for 35 to 40 minutes.

9 Serve the tamales immediately, alone, with the following Salsa Verde, or with Green Chile Sauce (see recipe, page 75). To eat, unwrap the husks or cut them open like a baked potato.

Makes 8 tamales

SALSA VERDE

1 pound	fresh tomatillos
1	small red onion, diced
2 cloves	fresh garlic, finely minced
2	serrano chiles, chopped
1 teaspoon	extra virgin olive oil
2 tablespoons	chopped fresh cilantro
½ teaspoon	fresh lime juice
	Salt and pepper, to taste

1 Peel the papery husks off the tomatillos and discard. Place the tomatillos in a steamer basket and steam for 10 to 15 minutes, or until soft.

2 Sauté the onion, garlic, and chiles in the olive oil over low heat so they caramelize, about 20 minutes.

3 Put the sautéed mixture plus cilantro and steamed tomatillos in the work bowl of a food processor and process until well puréed.

4 Add the lime juice, taste, then add salt and pepper to taste. Serve with Vegetarian Black Bean and Confetti Tamales.

Makes about 1 ½ cups

BUTTERNUT, VEGETABLE, AND PINQUITO BEAN SAUTÉ WITH PASILLA CHILE AND PUMPKIN SEED SAUCE

The pinquito bean, also known as the Santa Maria pinquito or the bush pin-quito, is grown in the Santa Barbara, Santa Maria, and San Luis Obispo areas. They were brought to this part of California via Mexico, by the Spaniards in the 1800s. The Dutch community of Solvang, near Santa Barbara, is one place you're sure to find pinquito beans on many restaurant menus. The beans are one of the few that retain their original color despite soaking and cooking. Their pinkish-brown hue adds so much to this colorful dish, as does their firm, round shape. These beans do not break up when cooked, so they are the structure of this "soft" vegetarian dish. If you cook this recipe using canned pinquitos, be sure to rinse them really well because they're often canned with sugar, which will wreak havoc with your digestive system.

You will always want to have a batch of this sauce around, so luckily it freezes well. Besides perfectly accenting any dark bean, and any winter squash, it is great with eggs, chicken, and roasted vegetables.

SAUTÉ

¾ cup	dried pinquito beans, soaked and drained, or one and a half 16-ounce cans, drained and well rinsed
One 3-inch piece	kombu seaweed
1 (about 1½ to 2 pound)	butternut squash
1	red onion, cut into quarters, then sliced crosswise
½	green bell pepper, cut into 1½-inch strips
½	red bell pepper, cut into 1½-inch strips
½	teaspoon dried basil
1 tablespoon	extra virgin olive oil
	Low-sodium soy sauce, to taste

SAUCE

2 tablespoons	pumpkin seeds
½	onion, diced
4 cloves	garlic, finely minced
One	8-ounce can whole tomatoes, plus juices
4	sundried tomatoes
1¼ cups	water
1 tablespoon	apple cider vinegar
2 tablespoons	dry red wine
½ cup	fresh cilantro leaves
¼ teaspoon	ground cumin
1½ teaspoons	pasilla chile powder (see Basics chapter, page xxii)
1 tablespoon	low-sodium soy sauce

1 Put the beans in a 3- or 4-quart saucepan. Add the kombu and enough water to cover by 2 inches. Cover, bring to a boil, reduce the heat to low, and simmer for 60 to 75 minutes, until the beans are tender. Remove and discard the kombu.

2 Meanwhile, bake the butternut squash at 350°F for 30 minutes only (it will not be completely baked at this point). Remove the butternut squash from the oven and let it cool. Peel, cut it in half lengthwise, and remove and discard the strings and seeds. Dice the squash and set it aside.

3 In a large sauté pan, sauté the onion, bell peppers, and basil in the olive oil over medium heat for 5 minutes. Add the cubed butternut squash and soy sauce and cook, covered, for 10 to 15 more minutes, or until the squash is tender throughout.

4 Drain the cooked beans, add to the sauté pan, cover, and cook for 5 minutes to blend flavors.

5 To make the sauce, preheat the oven to 325°F and toast the pumpkin seeds for 12 minutes. Remove from the oven and set aside.

6 Put the onion, garlic, tomatoes, sundried tomatoes, water, vinegar, and wine in a 3- or 4-quart saucepan. Bring to a boil, lower the heat, cover, and simmer for 15 minutes.

7 While the sauce is simmering, add the pumpkin seeds to the dry work bowl of a food processor and process to a powder.

8 When the sauce has cooked for 15 minutes, add the saucepan mixture to the food processor with the powdered pumpkin seeds, and purée again.

9 Add the cilantro leaves and purée well. Return the mixture to the saucepan.

10 Add the cumin, pasilla chile powder, and soy sauce to the sauce. Taste and add more chile powder, to your tolerance.

11 To serve, spoon butternut/bean sauté onto dinner plates and top with sauce. Serve hot.

Serves 8

BOLITA BEAN AND TURKEY TACOS WITH AVOCADO CREAM

Bolita beans were developed from the pinto by the Spanish who settled in northern New Mexico. To this day there are people in this area with strong opinions in the pinto-versus-bolita-bean debate. I heard of one family in Abiquiu, New Mexico, where the husband forbade his wife to cook pintos, insisting on the superiority of bolitas. Are they superior, or better? It's a matter of personal preference, but if you like a richer-tasting bean with more depth of flavor, you'd probably enjoy the bolita bean more.

In this recipe, I pair bolita beans with leftover turkey—something you always want a recipe for toward the end of November. For a quicker version, substitute a fifteen-ounce can of pinto (sorry!) or black beans for the home-cooked bolitas.

BEANS

¾ cup	bolita beans, soaked and drained
One 3-inch strip	kombu seaweed

TACOS

2 cloves	garlic, finely minced
1	small onion, sliced
½	red bell pepper, sliced
½	green bell pepper, sliced
2 teaspoons	chili powder
½ teaspoon	ground cumin
¼ teaspoon	dried oregano
¼ teaspoon	ground black pepper
1 tablespoon	extra virgin olive oil
One	8-ounce can tomatoes, plus juices
2 cups	leftover turkey, cubed or shredded

TO ASSEMBLE

6   corn tortillas
Vegetable oil spray as needed

AVOCADO CREAM

1   large avocado
2 tablespoons   nonfat plain yogurt
¼ teaspoon   ground cumin
Salt and pepper, to taste

1   Put the beans in a 3- or 4-quart saucepan. Add the kombu and enough water to cover by 2 inches. Cover, bring to a boil, reduce the heat to low, and simmer for 45 to 60 minutes, until the beans are tender. Remove and discard the kombu.

2   In a large sauté pan, sauté the garlic, onion, bell peppers, and spices in the olive oil over medium heat until the peppers are soft, about 10 minutes.

3   Add the drained and cooked beans, tomatoes, and turkey. Simmer, covered, for about 10 minutes.

4   Meanwhile, mash the avocado and stir in the yogurt. Season with the cumin, salt, and pepper. Taste, adjust the seasonings, and set aside.

5   Heat the tortillas by wrapping in moist paper towels and heating in the microwave, or spray a nonstick skillet lightly with vegetable oil spray and cook the tortillas, turning once, until limp.

6   Spoon the bean/turkey mixture in the middle of each tortilla. Top with avocado cream, and fold up like a taco. Secure with a toothpick and serve immediately. Serve salsa on the side for those who like it.

Makes 6 tacos

BORLOTTI BEANS AND NOODLES

Borlotti beans came to America from Italy, carried with care by immigrants to their new land. Imagine moving to a new country, with so many unknowns. Food has always been a source of comfort, an anchor for tradition, so I can see why someone thought to transport this bean—so important to Italian heritage—across the Atlantic to make this strange land feel a little more like home. This simple act of self-sufficiency provided security for generations as the seeds were saved, planted, harvested, cooked, and eaten year after year.

Borlottis, often called "improved cranberry beans," are big, plump beans, very creamy with a robust flavor. They are accented beautifully by the sweetness of onions, the herbal taste of sage and rosemary, and the slight acidity of the tomatoes in this humble dish.

2 cups	dried borlotti beans, soaked and drained
One 6-inch strip	kombu seaweed
1 stalk	celery, cut into chunks
1	carrot, cut into chunks
2 cloves	whole garlic
2	yellow onions, cut into quarters, then sliced crosswise
2 tablespoons	extra virgin olive oil
1 teaspoon	dried sage
1 teaspoon	minced fresh rosemary, or ½ teaspoon dried rosemary
2 cups	diced fresh tomatoes
½ teaspoon	salt
¼ cup	chopped fresh parsley (optional)
1 to 2 teaspoons	red wine vinegar
8 ounces	dried wide, flat noodles

1 Put the beans in an 8-quart Dutch oven. Add the kombu, celery, carrot, garlic, and enough water to cover the beans. Cover, bring to a boil,

reduce the heat to low, and simmer for 60 minutes, until the beans are tender. Remove and discard the kombu and vegetables.

2   Bring a large pot of water to a boil for the noodles.

3   Meanwhile, put the onions in a large sauté pan with the olive oil. Over medium heat, cook, uncovered, for about 20 minutes, or until the onions are sweet and golden in color.

4   Add the sage and rosemary to the sauté pan and cook, stirring well, for about 5 minutes.

5   Add the tomatoes, salt, parsley, if using, and vinegar and toss gently. Turn the heat off.

6   Cook the noodles until done, about 10 minutes. Drain and add to the onion/tomato mixture.

7   When the beans are done, drain them, and add to the onion/tomato/ noodle mixture. Toss well to mix, being careful not to break up the beans, tomatoes, or noodles. Serve immediately.

Serves 8

RATTLESNAKE BEANS WITH TOASTED SPICES AND SHERRIED TOMATOES

The Native Americans who farmed the land had ceremonies to mark and honor the seasonal cycles. Planting was a very spiritual undertaking. Among the Hopis, Kokopelli is the mythological character associated with fertility and germination. His image—a man with a hunchback playing the flute—has been found etched in stone and painted on pots throughout the continent, dating back centuries. The hump on his back is said to be a pack of seeds from which he plants as he moves around. The flute is said to be the source of the spirit breathed into every seed. Rattlesnake beans, ancient beans of the Southwest, were planted for years by the Hopi, sewn with the help of Kokopelli, who infused each seed with the spirit they so honored. Serve this full-flavored bean dish with the following Green Chile Rice and Almonds, plus a green salad for a complete meal.

2 cups	dried rattlesnake beans, soaked and drained
One 6-inch strip	kombu seaweed
2	carrots, cut into 3-inch chunks
½	yellow onion, quartered
2 whole cloves	garlic, peeled
1 teaspoon	salt
1 teaspoon	cumin seeds
1 teaspoon	coriander seeds
¼ cup	Sherried Tomato Paste (see Basics chapter, page xxiii)

1 Put the beans in a 3- or 4-quart saucepan. Add the kombu, carrots, onion, garlic, and enough water to cover by 2 inches. Cover, bring to a boil, reduce the heat to low, and simmer for 60 minutes, until the beans are tender. Remove and discard the kombu and vegetables. Stir in salt.

2 Meanwhile, toast the cumin seeds and coriander seeds in a dry skillet until fragrant, about 2 minutes. Remove from the heat immediately and grind in a spice grinder or with a mortar and pestle. This will equal 1 tablespoon of ground spices. (Alternately, measure out 1½ teaspoons

ground cumin and 1½ teaspoons ground coriander and toast briefly in a dry skillet.)

3 Stir the spices and Sherried Tomato Paste into the beans. Serve with Green Chile Rice and Almonds (see following recipe).

Serves 6 to 8

GREEN CHILE RICE AND ALMONDS

Even though the Green Chile Sauce described below is made with one of the mildest chiles available, the anaheim, be aware that it does have a little kick.

2 cups	water
1 cup	short- or long-grain brown rice, rinsed
1	bay leaf
¼ cup	slivered almonds

GREEN CHILE SAUCE

1	small red onion, diced
3 cloves	garlic, finely minced
½ tablespoon	olive oil
1 teaspoon	dried marjoram
1½ cups	roasted anaheim chiles, or three 3½-ounce cans Ortega chiles
2 cups	water
½ teaspoon	salt

1 Bring the water to a boil, slowly add the rice and bay leaf, cover, bring back to a boil, reduce the heat to low, and simmer for 30 to 35 minutes, or until the rice is tender.

2 Preheat the oven to 325°F and toast the almonds for 12 minutes, until light golden. Set aside.

3 Meanwhile, to make Green Chile Sauce, in a 3- or 4-quart saucepan sauté the onion and garlic in olive oil until the onion is transparent. Add the marjoram and cook 1 minute longer.

4 Add the chiles, water, and salt, bring to a boil, then simmer, uncovered, for 30 minutes, or until the juices begin to thicken.

5 Purée half the sauce, then return to the pot to keep warm.

6 When the rice is done, stir in Green Chile Sauce and toasted almonds.

Serves 6

RECOOKED PINTO BEAN TOSTADAS

These tostadas are made with my version of refried beans. Rather than deriving their flavor from refrying in lard, my version entails cooking the beans in a meaty mushroom vegetable stock, then recooking them, lid off, with a little oil and more stock, which reduces and intensifies as it cooks down, permeating the beans with concentrated flavors. Clearly, they are much more healthful than traditional refries, and you'll find them to be more flavorful as well. The stock recipe makes twice as much as you'll need for one batch of beans, so you can freeze the leftover for next time. If you don't have the time to make or defrost the stock, substitute canned chicken broth.

Pinto beans are one of the first beans to come to the western United States, introduced from Mexico, and are among the most common beans currently grown in the West. As such, they are the subject of much research at agricultural universities, where scientists crossbreed strains to improve yield and pest and disease resistance. For instance, Dr. Dermot P. Coyne of the University of Nebraska at Lincoln will release a new pinto this year called "Chase," which he developed at the request of many bean growers. It is a high yielder, and resistant to two serious diseases: rust and bacterial blight. He bred it using classic hybridization and selection methods, coding into its genes the resistance that will eliminate the need for chemical sprays. He told me that the original pinto bean was last grown in Idaho in the 1930s and early 1940s, although it is preserved in storage at Pullman, Washington, and Fort Collins, Colorado. They grow a crop of these beans once every ten years or so to preserve the stock. I'd love to taste that original bean—maybe they'll market a few next time they grow them out (hint, hint).

BEANS

2 cups	dried pinto beans, soaked and drained
One 6-inch strip	kombu seaweed
6 cups	Mushroom Vegetable Stock (see recipe, page 78)
4 cloves	garlic, finely minced

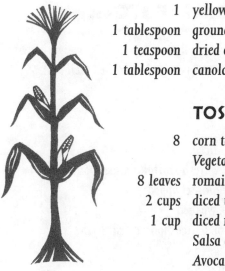

1	yellow onion, diced
1 tablespoon	ground cumin
1 teaspoon	dried oregano
1 tablespoon	canola oil

TOSTADAS

8	corn tortillas
	Vegetable oil spray as needed
8 leaves	romaine lettuce, cut into shreds
2 cups	diced tomatoes (optional)
1 cup	diced red onion or sliced green onions
	Salsa as needed
	Avocado Cream (see recipe, page 70)

1 Put the beans in a 3- or 4-quart saucepan. Add the kombu and Mush-room Vegetable Stock. Cover, bring to a boil, reduce the heat to low, and simmer for 60 minutes, until the beans are tender. Remove and discard the kombu. Drain off the stock, reserving 4 cups, and set aside.

2 Put the garlic, onion, spices, and canola oil in a large sauté pan. Sauté over medium heat until onion is transparent, about 5 minutes.

3 Add the salt and beans plus 1 cup stock to the sauté pan. Turn the heat to high and cook uncovered, stirring from time to time to prevent sticking. When the stock has evaporated, add more, 1 cup at a time, until the stock is almost gone, and the beans are very soft. Retain a little stock in the pan—the beans will soak it up as they sit to cool. Mash the beans with a potato masher or fork.

4 To cook tortillas, lightly spray a nonstick skillet or griddle with vegetable oil spray and cook the tortillas until crisp. Stack between paper towels.

5 To assemble tostadas, spread the recooked beans on each tortilla, then top with lettuce, tomatoes, onions, salsa, and Avocado Cream, as desired.

Serves 8

MUSHROOM VEGETABLE STOCK

1	large yellow onion, diced
	Dark green part of two leeks, washed well and sliced
3 stalks	celery, sliced
3	carrots, sliced
1	large tomato, diced
	Stems from 12 fresh shiitake mushrooms
10	white mushrooms, chopped
½ bunch	fresh cilantro, washed
Eight 4-inch sprigs	fresh thyme, or ½ teaspoon dried thyme
6 stems and leaves	fresh parsley
16	cups fresh water

1 Put all of the ingredients in a stockpot, cover, bring to a boil, turn the heat to low, and simmer for 1 hour.
2 Remove and discard the vegetables.
3 Store the stock, covered, in the refrigerator for up to 1 week, or freeze for up to 4 months.

Makes 2 quarts unsalted stock

GRILLED SALMON WITH RICE BEAN AND TOMATO WASABI RELISH

Rice beans are native to Asia, and are especially compatible with Asian flavors. Here I've used them in a salsa that contains two Japanese ingredients, miso and wasabi. Miso is a fermented soybean and rice paste with tremendous flavor and a dose of good bacteria that aids digestion. Wasabi is a tuberous, semiaquatic horseradish—actually an enlarged stem that grows in springwater. Wasabi was originally used as a natural preservative for raw fish—catch the fish, slice up the wasabi, and layer them together. One of the bean scientists I spoke with, Dr. Matt Silbernagle at Washington State University at Prosser, is at work establishing wasabi farms in Oregon and Washington. He said the subtleties of taste in a good, fresh wasabi is just like that of a good wine versus a bad wine. I look forward to tasting his cultivated wasabi some day. In the meantime, powdered wasabi or wasabi paste is what's available, and is used in this piquant bean salsa.

As discussed previously in "How to Silence Beans," serving beans with another protein food is a little hard on your digestive system. This is why I call for a small serving of fish with this spicy bean relish. See page xvii for a more thorough discussion.

BEANS AND RELISH

1 cup	dried rice beans, soaked and drained
One 3-inch strip	kombu seaweed
½	yellow onion, quartered
1 whole clove	garlic, peeled
1	carrot, cut into chunks
2	large yellow or red tomatoes, diced
1	small yellow onion, diced
½	red or orange bell pepper, diced
	Salt, to taste

WASABI VINAIGRETTE

¼ cup plus 2 tablespoons   canola oil

3 tablespoons   balsamic vinegar

2 teaspoons   mellow white miso

3 teaspoons   wasabi powder and 1½ teaspoons water (to make 1½ teaspoons paste)

1½ teaspoons   Oriental hot mustard powder

FISH

Eight   4-ounce salmon steaks

Vegetable oil spray as needed

1   Put the beans in a 3- or 4-quart saucepan. Add the kombu, onion, garlic, carrot, and enough water to cover by 2 inches. Cover, bring to a boil, reduce the heat to low, and simmer for 30 minutes, until the beans are tender yet still hold their shape. Remove and discard the kombu and vegetables.

2   Put the diced tomatoes, onion, and bell pepper in a medium-size mixing bowl. Drain the beans and add. Stir, taste, and season with salt.

3   Meanwhile, to make the vinaigrette, combine the oil, vinegar, and miso in a measuring cup or bowl. Mix the wasabi powder and water to make a paste and stir into vinaigrette. Stir in the hot mustard powder. Taste, and add more wasabi if needed. The beans will absorb plenty of the "hotness," so you might be able to add more.

4   Add 6 tablespoons vinaigrette to the bean relish. Stir well.

5   Preheat the oven to Broil. Lightly spray a wire rack with oil. Broil the salmon for 3 to 4 minutes per side. (You do not need to turn the fish if using a convection oven.)

6   To serve, place a portion of salmon on each of 8 dinner plates. Spoon on a teaspoon of wasabi vinaigrette. Top with the beans and relish, and serve immediately.

Serves 8

Oven-Baked Bean Main Dishes

GRATIN OF WINTER BEANS AND VEGETABLES

Unlike all other beans, the garbanzo is the only true winter crop, perfect for the cold-weather theme of this creamy gratin.

1	16-ounce can garbanzo beans, drained and rinsed
4 cloves	garlic, finely minced
½ teaspoon	dried thyme
3	eggs
3 cups	lowfat milk
½ teaspoon	salt
¼ teaspoon	black pepper
1 pound	potatoes, unpeeled and sliced ⅛ inch thick
½	large red onion, sliced ⅛ inch thick
½ pound	celeriac (celery root), peeled and sliced ⅛ inch thick
6 tablespoons	Parmesan cheese, grated

1   Preheat the oven to 350°F. Lightly spray an 8 x 8 x 2-inch baking dish with vegetable oil spray. Set aside.

2   Coarsely chop the garbanzo beans and toss them with the minced garlic and thyme. Set aside.

3   In a small bowl, whisk together the eggs, milk, salt, and pepper.

4   Lay half the potato slices in the baking dish, overlapping slightly. Add half the chopped garbanzo beans, half the onions, half the celeriac, then half the cheese.

5   Continue by layering the remaining potatoes, beans, onions, celeriac, and cheese.

6   Pour the milk/egg mixture over all.

7   Cover with foil and bake for 40 minutes.

8   Remove the foil and bake for an additional 35 to 40 minutes. Once during this period of baking, press down on the top layer of potatoes to coat them in the milk/egg mixture so they don't dry out. The gratin is done when it is bubbly and browned on top.

9   Remove from the oven and cool for about 15 minutes before serving. Serve warm.

Serves 12

CLAY-BAKED LEEKS AND CRANBERRY BEANS

The cranberry bean, like all members of the *Phaseolus* family, originated in the New World. Beginning in 1493 with the second voyage of Christopher Columbus, beans began their eastward voyage to the Old World, where they were enthusiastically received in Europe and Africa. Old World farmers took the American beans and bred them, producing many new bean varieties. The cranberry bean was brought back to the United States by Italian immigrants, and is now grown mostly on the California coast.

Here this creamy bean is combined with leeks and a miso-spiked broth, and baked in a clay pot commonly sold under the brand names of Schlemmertopf or Rommertopf. Baking in clay retains moisture, yet allows the foods inside to brown. In this instance, the beans remain smooth in texture, while the leeks soften and brown, lending a caramelized flavor to the dish. A clay baker is a wonderful way to cook chicken, and combinations of root vegetables like potatoes, parsnips, red onions, and rutabagas. You can substitute three-fourths cup chicken broth for the miso broth, if you prefer.

2 cups	dried cranberry beans, soaked and drained
One 6-inch strip	kombu seaweed
8	leeks, well washed
2 stalks	celery, cut into 3-inch chunks
1 whole clove	garlic
3 cloves	garlic, finely minced
1 tablespoon	extra virgin olive oil
2 teaspoons	mellow white miso

1   Put the beans in a 3- or 4-quart saucepan. Add the kombu, the green part of four of the leeks (save the white and light green parts), celery, whole clove of garlic, and enough water to cover by 2 inches. Cover, bring to a boil, reduce the heat to low, and simmer for 60 minutes, until the beans are tender yet still hold their shape. Remove and discard the kombu and vegetables.

2   Soak the lid of a 3-quart clay baker in cold water for 10 minutes, or according to the manufacturer's directions.

3   Slice the light green and white parts of the 8 leeks and place them, plus the minced garlic, in the bowl of the clay baker.

4 Drain the beans, saving ¾ cup bean water. Toss the beans with the leeks. Add the olive oil and miso to the bean water, mixing well. Pour this mixture over the beans and leeks.

5 Cover the clay baker with the soaked lid and place in a cold oven. Turn the heat to 350°F and bake for 1 hour.

6 Serve hot.

Serves 6

CURRIED LENTIL AND EGGPLANT CASSEROLE

Lentils are perhaps one of the oldest foods. They are mentioned in the Bible, and are said to be the source of strength and endurance of the Roman gladiators. Today the majority of United States lentils are grown in a small area of Washington and Idaho called the Palouse. Lentils were first introduced to this region around 1916, by a traveling, German-speaking, Seventh-Day Adventist minister named Schultz. The Seventh-Day Adventists were looking for a high-protein food to replace meat in their diet. Schultz gave a small quantity of lentil seed to J. J. Wagner of Farmington, Washington, to plant in his garden (Wagner's descendants are still farmers in this area). The lentils did quite well, so Wagner and two of his neighbors raised lentils for about ten years, finding a market for them among the Seventh-Day Adventists.

This nutritious food is also used as feed for chickens, cattle, sheep, and horses. A letter written in 1942 by a farmer extolling the virtues of growing lentils mentions their many advantages: they may be seeded earlier in the spring than most crops, they require little special machinery, they add nitrogen to the soil, and they control erosion better than peas and beans. The farmer then ventures into the culinary attributes of lentils, saying they are a "quick cooking dry food that can be used in such variety from soups, main dinner dish(es) to a tasty salad. Lentils cooked with other vegetables such as onions, tomatoes and peppers add great zest to the dish." I am in complete agreement. Serve this casserole with rice, tortillas, or pita bread. It improves with time, so leftovers are something to cheer about.

1 cup	dried green or brown lentils
One 3-inch strip	kombu seaweed
¼ teaspoon	salt
1	red onion, quartered, then sliced crosswise
1	red bell pepper, quartered lengthwise, then sliced crosswise
1 pound	eggplant, peeled and cut into 1-inch cubes
2 teaspoons	curry powder
⅛ teaspoon	cayenne

1 tablespoon	minced fresh ginger
1 tablespoon	extra virgin olive oil
¼ cup	dry red wine
One	28-ounce can whole tomatoes, plus juices
½ pound (about 2)	zucchini, sliced into rounds
	Yogurt Cheese (see Basics chapter, page xxiii) (optional)

1 Put the beans in a 3- or 4-quart saucepan. Add the kombu and enough water to cover by 2 inches. Cover, bring to a boil, reduce the heat to low, and simmer for 30 to 40 minutes, until the lentils are tender yet still hold their shape. Remove and discard the kombu. Add the salt, and set aside.

2 Preheat the oven to 325°F.

3 Add the onion, bell pepper, eggplant, curry powder, cayenne, ginger, and olive oil to a large sauté pan. Sauté over medium heat until the onion is transparent, about 5 minutes. When more liquid is needed, add the red wine.

4 Stir in the tomatoes, breaking them up as you add them.

5 Add the zucchini, then transfer to a 4-quart casserole. Cover and bake for 1½ hours. Let cool, then serve with rice or tortillas. Top with a dollop of Yogurt Cheese, if desired.

Serves 8

PAINTED PONY BEAN ENCHILADAS WITH RED CHILE SAUCE

The painted pony bean, also known as the brown mare bean, was probably developed from the appaloosa bean. Their shape and size are identical, and their markings are similar—painted ponies are just lighter overall in color. When I was a child, I must have had one of those pony-heads-on-a-stick with the same color combination as painted pony beans—every time I see one of these beans, I imagine felt ears and a goofy horse smile on them!

Purchase these beans exclusively from Zürsun Ltd. in Idaho, or substitute any of the appaloosa beans. The Red Chile Sauce relies on puréed vegetables rather than fat for its body. It is deeply flavored from the layering of tastes from vegetables and spices. Take note in the directions of the quick way to "cook" the spinach used as a filler ingredient for these luscious enchiladas.

BEANS

1 cup	painted pony beans, soaked and drained, or two 16-ounce cans black beans
One 3-inch strip	kombu seaweed
1 whole clove	garlic
½	yellow onion, quartered
1	carrot, cut into chunks
1 teaspoon	low-sodium soy sauce
1 teaspoon	ground cumin
Pinch	cayenne
4	scallions, sliced into rounds

SAUCE

6 cloves	garlic, finely minced
1½	red onions, diced
1 tablespoon	extra virgin olive oil
4 tablespoons	pasilla, ancho, guajillo, or New Mexico chile powder (see Basics chapter, page xxii)
2 tablespoons	ground cumin

2 teaspoons	dried oregano
1/2 teaspoon	salt
1/4 cup	dry sherry
1 tablespoon	low-sodium soy sauce
4	carrots, diced
One	28-ounce can whole tomatoes, plus juices
1 1/2 cups	water

TORTILLAS AND FILLERS

8 cups	spinach leaves, well washed
12	corn tortillas
	Vegetable oil spray as needed
1/4 pound	sharp cheddar cheese, grated
2	scallions, sliced into rounds

1 Put the soaked beans in a 3- or 4-quart saucepan. Add the kombu, garlic, onion, carrot, and enough water to cover by 2 inches. Cover, bring to a boil, reduce the heat to low, and simmer for 45 to 60 minutes, until the beans are tender. Remove and discard the kombu and vegetables. Or, rinse the canned beans, and proceed to next step.

2 Slightly mash the beans, and add the soy sauce, cumin, cayenne, and sliced scallions. Taste, and adjust the seasonings. Set aside.

3 Meanwhile, to make the sauce, put the garlic, onion, and oil in a 3- or 4-quart saucepan and sauté over medium heat until the onions are transparent, about 5 minutes.

4 Add the remaining ingredients, cover, bring to a boil, reduce the heat, and simmer for 20 to 30 minutes, or until the carrots are soft.

5 Put the sauce in the work bowl of a food processor and purée. Return to the saucepan.

6 When ready to assemble the enchiladas, preheat the oven to 350°F.

7 To "cook" the spinach, put it in a colander in the sink. Bring a pot or kettle of water to a boil and pour the boiling water over the spinach in the colander.

8 Coat the bottom of a 9 x 12-inch baking pan with a few ladlesful of sauce.

9 Rinse each tortilla with water. Heat the tortillas in a nonstick skillet until they are limp. (You may need to lightly spray the pan once with vegetable oil spray so the tortillas won't initially stick.) If you are going to freeze the enchiladas, spray each tortilla with vegetable oil spray before cooking, instead of rinsing in water.

10 Coat each warm tortilla with sauce. Fill the center with a strip of beans, a bit of cheddar cheese, spinach, and a spoonful of sauce. Roll and place each in the baking pan. Continue with each tortilla. Spread sauce over the top of the enchiladas, sprinkle on scallions, cover with foil and bake for 30 minutes. Serve immediately. Or freeze, then bake frozen enchiladas for 50 to 60 minutes at 350°F.

Serves 6 to 12

SOURCES FOR BEANS AND SEEDS

To find the beans used in the recipes in this book, check your local specialty stores, kitchen shops, ethnic stores, and natural food stores, or contact the following mail-order sources.

Adobe Milling Co., Inc.
P.O. Box 596
535 East Highway 666
Dove Creek, CO 81324
(303) 677–2620, (800) 54-ADOBE
Fax: (303) 677–2667

The Bean Bag
818 Jefferson Street
Oakland, CA 94607
(510) 839–8988
Fax: (510) 791–0705

Dean & DeLuca
560 Broadway
New York, NY 10012
(212) 431–1691, (800) 221–7714

Gallina Canyon Ranch
P.O. Box 706
Abiquiu, NM 87510
Send SASE + $1 for catalog.

Native Seeds/SEARCH
2509 N. Campbell Avenue #325
Tucson, AZ 85719
(602) 327–9123

Phipps Ranch
P.O. Box 349
Pescadero, CA 94060
(415) 879–0787

G. B. Ratto & Company
821 Washington Street
Oakland, CA 94607
(510) 832–6503, (800) 325–3483
Fax: (510) 836–2250

Seed Savers Exchange
3076 N. Winn Road
Decorah, IA 52101

Seeds of Change
621 Old Santa Fe Trail #10
Santa Fe, NM 87501
(505) 983–8956

Zürsun Ltd.
P.O. Box 4569
Ketchum, ID 83340
(208) 726–8881

INDEX